Discover *the* Editor *in* You

Forthcoming from Indian Copyeditors Forum (ICF)

Beyond Discovery: The Copyeditor's Handbook
All About Working as a Freelance Editor
Finding Your Editorial Niche

Discover *the* Editor *in* You

Copyediting as a career

Curated by
VIVEK KUMAR
for Indian Copyeditors Forum (ICF)

Editorial Committee

Abha Thapalyal Gandhi (Chair)
Anupam Choudhury
Murugaraj Shanmugam
Preeta Priyamvada

authors
UPFRONT

First published in India in 2023 by AuthorsUpFront
info@authorsupfront.com

ISBN: 978-93-94887-31-2

Printed at Saurabh Printers, Greater Noida, Uttar Pradesh

To all those copyeditors who keep on working tirelessly and remain away from the limelight

Contents

PART III: Technique and Craft

PART IV: Allied Services

Foreword

'Communication' as a field of study has always fascinated me because of its vastness, subtle nuances, and complexities. Communication encompasses all walks of life. And the techniques and technologies associated with it have kept evolving ever since human beings started speaking and writing to convey their thoughts.

Even as the technologies, techniques, and modes of communication constantly evolve and speed up the communication process, the basic process of communication remains the same and has the following main elements: (a) the sender, who originates the message; (b) the channel(s) through which the message is sent; (c) the noise, the undesirable or unwanted signals that get added to the original message; and (d) the recipient(s), who decodes the message. One may also add the response of the recipient, an analysis of which would tell us how 'effective' the communication was.

Therefore, for communication to be effective, the noise has to be reduced, even if it cannot be eliminated. Especially the controllable aspects of noise. Broadly, a copyeditor's job is to minimize the noise in the message. The chapters in this book – written by established communicators and editors in their respective fields – beautifully capture the noise elements of various nature and suggest ways and means to circumvent them effectively.

The practical insights and meticulously crafted narratives provided by these authors will indeed go a long way towards attracting young minds to this field.

Apart from demystifying the art of copyediting, this book, as a good teacher does, will handhold and lead young copyeditors to a number of learning resources and opportunities in this profession. Well, I was fortunate to have such a fabulous teacher (Yateendra Joshi) at the start of my career. I am happy to note that Yateen, as we fondly call him, has written two chapters in this very book!

Over the years, I have observed editors and learned about their temperament. If I can use a cricket analogy, some people's temperament may be good for a T20 game or one-day cricket or a test match. Temperament is something that young editors can and should find out for themselves. Accordingly, they can choose their niche in editing.

In other words, if your temperament works well for a shorter duration, you may choose your career in mass media where quick turnaround is expected. If you can sustain your temperament for a slightly longer duration, you may serve better as a journal editor or in a magazine. And if you can sustain it for a longer time, you may go for book editing. But once you gain experience, temperament can always be improved or adjusted for the task at hand.

The industry needs various types of skilled editors due to the ever-increasing platforms such as traditional publishing and online/digital publishing. A simple Google search for 'growth of publishing industry' indicated nothing but a positive trend. With much content being generated in the world every minute, copyediting or copyeditors become an indispensable check-post to enhance the 'effectiveness' quotient.

If you are the type who enjoys the journey more than the destination itself, copyediting is definitely a great career option. And you don't have to stop at being a copyeditor! You can spice it up by being a little bold by venturing into uncharted territories within this broad landscape of publishing or communication. The career graph of some of the chapter authors of this book can really inspire young editors like you as you plot your own career path.

- Murugaraj Shanmugam is an entrepreneur now, offering editorial services and training.
- Venkataraman Anantharaman, better known as Venkat in the publishing circle, runs a training institution now.
- Venkatesh Krishnamoorthy is busy as ever as a freelance editor but graduated as a writer as well now.
- Victoria Bell, a certified professional editor of scholarly text, is also a freelance copyeditor of fiction! What a shift!
- Reena Singh appears to have attained salvation after 'sprinting' for 38 years in a leading mass media institution in India and now runs a spiritual and wellness website!
- Yateendra Joshi stayed the course as an editor (one of the finest that I have seen) and has been training editors and researchers for a long time now. A walking encyclopaedia on STM editing, Yateen has also authored a book titled *Communicating in Style*.
- Ellen Sue Feld wears multiple hats, having acquired the ability to switch from one to another seamlessly.
- Sayantani De has moved from editing to entrepreneurship in the field of communication.
- Visalakshy Loganathan, a prolific copyeditor, is another entrepreneur and has widened her net beyond editorial services too.
- P K Jayanthan was a colleague of mine at The Energy and Resources Institute (TERI). He took a career shift at the fag end of his work life in TERI and got into copyediting and indexing! Ever since, he has been passionately wedded to these areas of work.

Vivek Kumar, the curator of this book, needs special mention. Apart from being a passionate copyeditor, Vivek attempted to do the 'unthinkable' about a decade ago – that of bringing publishing professionals under one roof called the ICF! He has succeeded in doing so too. Not only has he made ICF members active in the social media platforms that he has created for ICF, but he got some of them to write for this book as well. Kudos to him!

All of these examples show that copyediting could just be a beginning for you. And this book will serve as a golden key that opens you up to the possibilities not necessarily in copyediting but in other editorial roles as well.

Happy learning!

K P Eashwar

Preface

I have always been motivated by a snippet I once read in a newspaper: "taking India's best to the world and bringing the world's best to India". So, how did I translate this philosophy into reality? "Very few people know about copyediting. It would be great to have a book on copyediting," I thought to myself. The year was 2009. LinkedIn groups used to be very active at the time, and I floated the idea in several LinkedIn groups and received an overwhelming response from all over the world. Even a few chapters were written, but my full-time job (and a 5-hour commute), lack of experience with the publishing process, and lack of team members for the project left little time for me to pursue the authors and look for a publisher.

In 2016, I tried again to get the book going but the time was not ripe yet. In 2021, I floated the idea one more time and the end is now in sight – third time lucky! We set up a four-member editorial committee with Abha Thapalyal Gandhi as the chair and Anupam Choudhury, Murugaraj Shanmugam, and Preeta Priyamvada as members. The committee reviewed and approved proposals (sometimes reviewed even revised proposals), peer-reviewed each chapter twice (at times even three times), helped authors with surveys and questionnaires, sent regular progress bulletins, and remained in contact through WhatsApp chats, phone calls, and video calls.

Most of the authors are also from ICF (Indian Copyeditors Forum) and are specialists in their respective fields. For some sections in the book (e.g. credentials in copyediting and allied services), I wrote to editing associations in the United Kingdom and Canada and they responded graciously and agreed to contribute chapters. I see endless possibilities of collaboration (cross-training), growth, and compounding because of the multi-person effort that this project grew into. These possibilities do not arise when working alone.

Discover the Editor in You: copyediting as a career is targeted at graduates and postgraduates who are looking for an offbeat yet attractive career option that has the potential to not only satisfy their creative urge, but is also recession-proof – a career that can provide the option of working from home or from anywhere in the world, for organizations in India and abroad. *Discover the Editor in You* looks at the numerous possibilities that a career in copyediting has to offer.

- If you have a good command of English, can explain your edits to writers, can give the job at hand close attention over long periods, have an eye for detail, and can communicate effectively, you can be a good copyeditor.
- If you want to read literature or research journals for free, then be a copyeditor because you will get to work on journals or books about cutting-edge research from many disciplines.
- If you are a problem solver and disciplined, then be a copyeditor to help content creators to tighten and focus their output.

Copyediting has become particularly important ever since firms engaged in business-process outsourcing and knowledge-process outsourcing came into being because of the outsourcing wave by international (especially American) companies and publishers.

Unlike the copyediting guides available in the market, most of which are solo efforts by foreign authors, *Discover the Editor in You* has deliberately been designed to be a multi-author effort in which people from India and abroad have written chapters on different facets of copyediting in their area of expertise so that the reader gets to read the best. The book is a unique compendium of studies, experiences, and guidelines on copyediting for a global readership.

Discover the Editor in You addresses in detail the tremendous change that technology has brought about in the field of copyediting so that the reader feels well equipped and confident to work with any style of copyediting.

The initial part of the book deals with all the issues and elements that copyediting as a career involves, whereas the later parts explain to beginners in the field what they will have to deal with as copyeditors and how best they can address those matters.

Members of the ICF have helped us put together India's first multi-authored book on copyediting, a wonderful career choice that unfortunately so few people know about. We hope this book (and other books the ICF hopes to publish) will be the stepping stones to success not only for India's young and bright minds straight out of college but also for those thinking of transitioning into copyediting from other industries. ICF has fulfilled my dream with the publication of this book, and I hope it will fulfil yours too.

About Indian Copyeditors Forum

A Note From the Founder

June 2015 was an extremely memorable month for me. In 2014, when I joined the Facebook group Editors' Association of Earth (EAE), I came to know about the first international conference for editors being organized by the Editors' Association of Canada (now Editors Canada) in June 2015. Major editing associations from countries across the world were participating, but I was sorry to see that India would not be represented although it is the second-largest English-language book market in the world. I got in touch with my mentor Anantharaman Venkataraman (Dr Venkat) and requested him to submit a proposal for a presentation at the conference. He agreed, and his proposal was accepted. Next, I got in touch with Sunita Dogra, my ex-colleague at Aptara. She too happily agreed to come along for the conference, and we, the three musketeers (who would be meeting after years in a foreign land), were all set to have a great time in Toronto, Canada. But life has never been easy for me. My application for the visa was rejected, and I had to apply again; Sunita too was worried whether she would be granted one. But she got her visa without any hiccups, and the three of us met on the morning of the conference. We met so many editors we had known only online and divided the sessions on offer among ourselves so that we could cover them all and compare notes later. Those three days were the best days of my life.

Once I was back in India, I was determined to start a group for editing professionals in India. Starting a Facebook group seemed the easiest thing to do, and I created Indian Copyeditors Forum: The Forum for Editors[1] (ICF) on 28 June 2015 and added my editor friends and colleagues as the first few members who in turn added others they knew.

ICF is an informal Facebook group for Indian editors who edit in English (https://www.facebook.com/groups/Indianeditors), and its aim is to share knowledge, ideas, thoughts, and resources among the editorial community. The group has 2847 members as of 1 June 2023.

All these years we were trying to build a critical mass, and with this book we hope to reach that.

The lack of formal registration has not stopped us from conducting meetings, workshops, and webinars. In fact, Visalakshy Loganathan, one of our members and also the author of the chapter on alt text writing in this book, was gutsy enough to organize India's first conclave for copyeditors in Chennai in February 2018. We have published newsletters, and we even have a website with a blog that has pieces by some of the world's best editors. We have a volunteer team running our Twitter handle, and a team of volunteers helped us run a weekend webinar series for more than a year during the COVID period. We are on Clubhouse, LinkedIn, and Pinterest. We hope a young member will soon represent us on Instagram too. And we hope to have a Wikipedia page and an app too.

Vivek Kumar

---

1 Many people have asked me whether the forum's name should have an apostrophe. To be honest, I never gave this a thought when I was busy setting up the group. Now, when I look back, I realize that apostrophes present all sorts of problems when it comes to branding, marketing, and other related matters. Omitting the apostrophe is simply cleaner: the Authors Guild or the Editorial Freelancers Association or the Freelancers Union – all are best without it.

Introduction

Publishing and the Profession of Copyediting Today

Abha Thapalyal Gandhi

A good editor is someone who cares a little less about the author's needs than the reader's.

– Dene October[1]

People who are not familiar with the work of a copyeditor often wonder what all the fuss is about. They also ask, quite legitimately, why an editor is allowed to interfere with an author's creation. Even within publishing companies, editors may find themselves at the receiving end of sceptical questioning by colleagues from other departments. So, it may come as a surprise to many that today, when we are in the third decade of the 21st century, the role of copyeditors has only grown in the publishing business worldwide as well as in a number of other fields of work.

The information technology revolution that swept the advanced countries of the world in the last two decades of the 20th century, and India in the first two of the 21st, turned many jobs into dinosaurs. However, it can be said confidently that people who worked with words adapted marvellously. Typewriters disappeared, but typists did not! Many of us can recall the changing look and sound of offices

1 October (2008)

as silent, dumpy-looking personal computers began replacing the persistent clickety-clack of typewriters. It was no longer necessary to make and pass on faded fourth, fifth, and sixth 'carbon copies' to hapless recipients. Far more legible computer printouts became the order of the day.

ADAPTING TO TECHNOLOGY

Large numbers of the scholarly and literary minded, including of course professionals in the natural and social sciences, also began using computers. They adapted themselves to 'word processing' and other useful 'software', while remaining focused on their core competencies – study, research, and communicating through words. Whatever changes the information technology storm brought, the scope for editorial work grew regardless. During the same period, from the late 1990s to the early 2000s, as the internet became increasingly more effective and accessible, India firmly established itself as a hub for a large amount of 'processing' work for global publishing businesses, especially in the scientific, technical, and medical (STM) segments. The work ranged from data conversion, typesetting, and the full range of pre-press work to lower- and mid-level editorial tasks. The flurry of contract assignments was so great, and the results for early-bird outsourcing companies so advantageous, that by 2011 India was receiving about 60% of the global outsourced publishing business (Mallya 2011).

Because of the explosive growth of information technology, new digital platforms became available to governmental, commercial, and social entities, as well as to individuals, for public information and marketing purposes. As anyone who has ever stopped to think about words and communication realizes, effective marketing cannot happen without a clear understanding of the vocabulary as well as thought processes of the intended consumer, nor can information be communicated meaningfully. The result was that more and more writing was being done or, to use the currently favoured term, more and more 'content' was being created. A new set of businesses that needed quality content realized the value of a unique set of professionals – people who could understand the importance of using the appropriate word for a particular situation and could supply that word, who could extract sense out of confused and confusing grammar, rewrite whole lines where necessary, help develop a clear message, and, ultimately, link content creators with their audiences.

ESSENTIAL CONCEPTS IN EDITING

While significant changes have occurred in the editorial profession in India, it should be emphasized that certain critical concepts at the heart of copyediting remain untouched, and aspiring copyeditors need to understand them to get a grip on editorial work and to mature as professionals.

Ensuring clarity of expression

Good writing requires three things, namely clarity of thought, a thorough grounding in the rules of a language, and effective use of words, meaning that any piece of writing should be appropriate in itself as well as for its target audience. The essential role of a copyeditor is that of a dispassionate observer who assesses whether the author's message is getting through and, if not, figures out why not.

When written work is not finalized carefully, confusion can occur. Once a book or article is published, a report circulated, a brochure distributed, or any written material has gone beyond the author's or publisher's control, making changes ceases to be a simple matter. What a good copyeditor needs to be on the lookout for are issues of grammar, logic, continuity, appropriateness of vocabulary, and consistency of style. That is no doubt a lot of ground to cover. Errors in grammar and usage, particularly, take away the clarity and elegance of a piece of writing.

- He noticed a number of well-preserved and beautifully framed theatre posters walking down the stairs.
- A number of video clips supposedly of authentic scenes of public protests were reported to have been tampered with by a forensic lab.
- The melancholy young man who lived next door stopped attending church since two years.
- Three overconfident classmates of mine failed the mid-terms because they did not studied seriously.

The first two sentences contain interesting facts and arouse the reader's curiosity, but each also creates ambiguity or a surreal absurdity regarding the action referred to. Who was walking downstairs, the theatre posters or 'he'? In the second sentence, one is left wondering whether the lab itself tampered with the videos! The first two examples contain a 'dangling participle', which is a modifier, but it is not clear which noun or pronoun it modifies. In the third sentence, the reference is to a period, not a particular time such as a date, month, or year. So instead of 'since' one could say 'two years ago' or 'for two years', depending on the context. The last sentence is a negative statement in the simple past tense, which means that the main verb must remain in its base form, 'study'.

Copyeditors need to understand every single word and expression they read and should make changes only when they are sure they do. For example, the words 'decry', 'denigrate', and 'deprecate' are listed as synonyms in standard dictionaries, yet there are differences and shades of meaning that need to be thought about before the most appropriate term can be chosen. Homonyms can also be challenging. It would be unforgiveable, for example, to change 'gaol' to 'goal' or 'reek' to 'wreak' or 'compliment' to 'complement'. Verbosity is yet another enemy of good writing and editing. Copyeditors need to be alert to phrases such as 'untrue defamatory claims', 'a divine godly appearance', 'a chilling cold stare', or 'a heated angry argument' and sentences such as 'He had always been an early riser from his student days, getting up very early in the morning'.

Thus, the essential task of a copyeditor is to ensure that the author's message is clear, grammatically correct, and written in a way that is understandable and convincing to the intended audience. A wonderfully picturesque description of what copyeditors do is provided by a senior journalist and editor who worked with the *New York Times* for many years (Downes 2008):

> They untangle twisted prose. They are surgeons, removing growths of error and irrelevance; they are minimalist chefs, straining fat. . . . The copy editor's job, to the extent possible under deadline, is to slow down, think things through, do the math and ask the irritating question.

The 'author's voice' and the author–editor relationship

The concept of 'voice' includes a range of concerns from the choice of words and the complexity or otherwise of sentences to emotions and values. 'The author's voice directly reflects the attitude of the author himself' (Literary Terms, n.d., literaryterms.net/voice/). In other words, the author's voice reveals the author's personality, which is something no one is permitted to eclipse.

It is well worth remembering that the author and the editor are collaborators or partners. Editors have been thanked in the acknowledgement pages of innumerable books on every possible subject. For instance, in *Scattered Minds: a new look at the origins and healing of attention deficit disorder*, the psychologist-author, Gabor Maté, warmly acknowledges the copyeditor, Alison Reid, for her "expert and attentive work greatly enhanced the flow of the text without in any way detracting from its meaning" (Maté 1999).

In the days when publishing businesses were owned by families and individuals, there were schedules and plans, no doubt, but one may say with confidence that the overall pace was slower. Most editors worked in-house and regularly engaged with authors. Their work was more akin to that of contemporary 'developmental editors'. The most extraordinary of them actively influenced the development of important literary works. One remarkable example is the interaction between Harper Lee, author of the modern American classic *To Kill a Mockingbird*, and her editor, Tay Hohoff. The book was published in 1960; when a posthumous work, *Go Set a Watchman*, was published 55 years later, it turned out that it was not a new novel at all but the first draft of the powerful and hugely popular 1960 novel – a draft that had been very significantly altered by the author on the basis of suggestions made by her editor (Neary 2015).

Possibly the most famous English-language editor of the 20th century was Maxwell Perkins, who can truly be described as a legend. His name will always be connected to some of the great American novelists, including F Scott Fitzgerald, Thomas Wolfe, and Ernest Hemingway. His intense involvement with his authors is vividly and unforgettably described by his biographer, A Scott Berg (1978):

> More a friend to his authors than a taskmaster, he aided them in every way. He helped them structure their books, if help was needed; thought up titles, invented plots; he served as psychoanalyst, lovelorn advisor, marriage counsellor, career manager, money-lender. Few editors before him had done so much work on manuscripts, yet he was always faithful to his credo, "The book belongs to the author."

CORPORATIZATION OF THE PUBLISHING BUSINESS

The author–editor collaboration and intellectual exchange will always be important, especially in the field of literature. The ground reality in the current period, however, is that there is considerable pressure to find potential 'best sellers'. As part of their routine, commissioning or product editors at publishing houses are expected to focus their attention, and obviously time, on sales and marketing, apart from their traditional work. This trend began when the major publishing houses in North America and Europe were taken over by corporate entities or other publishers who themselves were on the way to becoming behemoths, mostly in the last part of the 20th century. The guiding force then became what has been criticized as 'hyper commercialization' in which the priority was the bottom line – in other words, corporate profits.

Significantly, after the mergers or acquisitions, the names (imprints) of all the old publishers were retained because of their well-established goodwill, which also perhaps added a touch of old-world lustre to the profits being made. Companies continue to be bought and sold in the present century. So, McGraw Hill Education, which used to be owned by Apollo Global Management, was sold in 2021 to Platinum Equity; HarperCollins is a subsidiary of News Corporation; Macmillan Publishers is a subsidiary of Holtzbrinck Publishing Group; Simon & Schuster is a subsidiary of ViacomCBS; Routledge was acquired by Taylor & Francis, which is in turn owned by Informa UK Ltd; Penguin and Random House have merged and are jointly owned by Bertelsmann, a German media company, and Pearson, the publishers. Doubleday, Viking, Alfred Knopf, Hamish Hamilton, and Jonathan Cape all belong to the Bertelsmann group.

Global outsourcing of publishing work

One of the exigencies of business is the need to keep expenses as low as feasible and the profits as high as possible. When the internet and its capabilities began to be understood in the United States and Europe during the 1980s and 1990s, large publishing houses and corporations realized that there was an unprecedented opportunity for them. It became realistic to think of hiring professionals – typesetters, data converters, designers, and editors – in faraway low-wage locations. So began the global outsourcing of huge chunks of the publishing business, mentioned earlier in this essay.

Division of editorial tasks

With the corporate takeovers of publishing businesses, the way of doing editorial work also changed significantly. Serious editors in the past could be described as all-rounders who did an overall analysis as well as a deep-dive study. They analysed writing in terms of its structure, the logic and impact of the narrative, the quality of language, the freshness of the content, and so on. They sat with their red and blue pencils and physically marked up scripts. With schedules becoming more demanding and market pressures increasing, it seems accurate to say that publishers were no longer willing to allow in-house editors to edit whole manuscripts. The way forward was to turn these professionals into 'editorial managers' or 'desk editors' who would develop a network of freelancers to do the actual editing.

In keeping with the modern world's penchant for specialization, division of tasks according to the complexity involved and, most of all, for fast execution, editorial work too was broken down into components and no longer remained a comprehensive exercise. Editors senior in age and experience have been known to report that it took them time, years in fact, to realize that the editorial interventions they routinely made and conversations they engaged in with authors were actually 'developmental' or 'structural' editing, not merely 'copyediting'.

The broken-down and standardized tasks carried out in publishing work outsourced to India definitely had a logic and their execution has been very successful, especially in the STM segment. Many publishing tasks have become increasingly technical and dependent on various software packages, which is another reason that several different professionals work on the finalization of each manuscript. Tasks that are outsourced and carried out by different sets of employees include plagiarism checks, fact checks, tagging, subject indexing, keyword indexing, basic language editing, mechanical editing, and implementation of the relevant style guide. One social scientist in the United States, after studying outsourced publishing businesses for a year, calculated that each journal article accepted by a publisher using the outsourced model 'passes across the desktop computers of between 40 and 50 front-line employees in the global South' (Sallaz 2013).

It must be pointed out that higher level editorial work in all areas requires more than a grasp of grammar and does not lend itself to being carved up into tasks and, so far, is not being outsourced. While editorial work is detail oriented, it also requires one to have clarity about the overall message and concerns of the text – the story, novel, report, article, thesis, or whatever kind of writing one is working on. Most significantly in the context of outsourced businesses, editing requires one to have a nuanced understanding of the culture and language of the place where the manuscript comes from.

Significantly, outsourcing editorial work in areas such as non-fiction, literary fiction, marketing collateral, and trade magazines has proven to be a complicated matter with less satisfactory outcomes than in the various fields of STM. It is not surprising to learn that a predominant view among publishers abroad is that 'editing services are especially problematic when outsourced offshore' (Fersht and Filippone 2013). Any experienced editor reading such comments knows that, in India at least, there are plenty of editors who can handle the more sophisticated levels of editing. However, such professionals are not the kind who apply for low-paid jobs offered by companies doing outsourced publishing.

LOOKING AHEAD

To sum up, it is true that a variety of editorial interventions will continue to be required as long as people write and that opportunities for work will keep on growing, but the environment is complex. From the publishers to those handling KPOs or BPOs (knowledge-process outsourcing or business-process outsourcing), from individual authors in India and abroad to the news media, from government bodies to website operators, and a whole host of others, there are many sources of work. The challenge for novice editors today is finding their niche: work they are good at, the kind that they can spend hours on each day, and, equally important, has the potential to provide them with the income that they aspire to.

On the principle of 'forewarned is forearmed', the aim of this little book is to provide novice editors, and others considering joining the profession, with a realistic idea of what copyediting and some allied editorial tasks involve today, as well as the insights of experienced professionals. While perfection is not to be had in this world and we certainly cannot lay claim to it, we do hope that *Discover the Editor in You* to some extent fulfils its purpose and proves to be of value to its readers.

REFERENCES

Berg A S. 1978. *Max Perkins: editor of genius*, p. 4. New York: New American Library (Penguin Random House). 512 pp.

Downes L. 2008. In a changing world of news, an elegy for copy editors. *The New York Times*, 16 June. https://www.nytimes.com/2008/06/16/opinion/16mon4.html

Fersht P and Filippone T. 2013. *The Sourcing Industry Blueprint 2.0*, p. 27. https://globaldialogue.isa-sociology.org/uploads/imgen/1429-v3i4-english.pdf

Mallya V. 2011. Dotting the 'i' of Indian publishing. *Logos* **22** (1): 37–46

Maté G. 1999. *Scattered Minds: a new look at the origins and healing of attention deficit disorder*. London: Vermilion. 348 pp.

Neary L. 2015. What exactly does an editor do? The role has changed over time, *Books News and Features*, 29 December. https://tinyurl.com/roleofeditor

October D.[2] 2008. www.goodreads.com/quotes/tag/editor

Sallaz J J. 2013. Your paper has just been outsourced. *Global Dialogue* **3** (4): 17–19

---

2 Goodreads not being the original source, we asked Dene October about the exact source, and he responded as follows (on 4 March 2023, by email):

> "I don't have a clear reference I can give you. I used to say this kind of thing a lot in Writing Design classes back sometime in the 2000s. Something like, 'there are two types of editor: one steps out in front of you while you are writing carrying a big red stop sign. Push them away, they're blocking your progress, even if they claim to be acting in your interest. The other editor only appears after your first draft. Embrace them, they're freeing up your access to the reader. A good editor is someone who cares a little less about the author's needs than the reader's'. Some of this was up on line for a while, on University blogs and forums, things like Blackboard, etc. This is where it must have got picked up by someone and quoted the first time. I can see the first mention on Goodreads is in 2008 (I didn't join Goodreads until the mid teens when I discovered it). It has subsequently been re-quoted a lot, including self-consciously by me in 2018 when I was thanking the editors of the Marco Polo book! I realise doesn't help your bibliography question – it seems memes hate origins!"

PART I

Becoming a Copyeditor

CHAPTER 1

Who Is a Copyeditor?

Necessary Skills and Mindset

Murugaraj Shanmugam

Before the printing press was invented in the 15th century, Europe produced about a hundred books every year, or about 10,000 books in one hundred years. By 1950, nearly five centuries later, Europe was publishing 10,000 books a month: what once took a century took only one month. At the time of writing this chapter (June 2022), more than 275,000 books are published each year worldwide, averaging 753 books every day, or 31 books every hour (Bowker n.d., as cited in Bloomsbury Review; www.bloomsburyreview.com/getreviewed.html). And almost all these books, no matter which format they are in, are being checked by a copyeditor.

Never before has the world needed a copyeditor more desperately than now!

DOES AN AUTHOR MAKE MISTAKES?

Each author is unique. Some authors are equally proficient both in their subject and in the language in which they write. Such authors rarely face any challenges in communicating their ideas and thoughts coherently, and their readers hardly encounter any difficulties while reading. Works of such authors demand little intervention from copyeditors other than fixing mundane typographical errors and making the manuscript compliant with the publisher's guidelines. Usually called 'specs', short for specifications, these guidelines include instructions on various aspects of typesetting a book, including guidelines for copyediting.

Many other authors struggle to express their ideas or fail to translate their thoughts into comprehensible text. These shortcomings may arise from the authors' inadequate command of language. As a result, the text may suffer from a wrong choice of words or faulty syntax, which often leads to misinterpretation. Such lapses in communication are less conspicuous: whereas slips in denotations are easy to identify, spotting any flaws in conveying the intended meaning may require additional skills.

Some authors possess an enviable command over their subject but not over language. These authors often find it difficult to share their expertise with others through the written text: language becomes a stumbling block for them in conveying their ideas intelligibly to readers, with ambiguous and unclear sentences greatly limiting comprehension.

WHO IS A COPYEDITOR?

When authors fall short in expressing their ideas or when language becomes a stumbling block, copyediting and therefore copyeditors play an inevitable role. But what is that role? We need to define it more distinctly. Comprehending who a copyeditor is will strengthen our understanding of the importance of a copyeditor in the publishing world.

The Chicago Manual of Style – hailed as the bible for copyeditors – states that copyediting encompasses "simple mechanical corrections (mechanical editing) through sentence-level interventions (line, or stylistic, editing) to substantial remedial work on literary style and clarity, disorganized passages, baggy prose, muddled tables and figures, and the like (substantive editing)" (Einsohn and Schawartz 2019). This description of copyediting is formal and talks about the interplay between the copyeditor and the text, touching upon the various levels of interventions a text can be subjected to by the copyeditor.

Butcher's Copy-editing aptly captures the essence of copyediting by acknowledging the dynamic role of the copyeditor (Butcher, Drake, and Leach 2006), stating that copyediting seeks "to remove any obstacles between the reader and what the author wants to convey and to find and solve any problems before the book goes to the typesetter, so that production can go ahead without interruption or unnecessary expense". A copyeditor, thus, functions as a bridge that connects the author and the reader and helps authors to communicate their thoughts better to the reader.

The notable Tamil writer Jeyamohan, while writing about copyediting of publications in Tamil, succinctly captures the reason why authors make mistakes and how copyeditors help authors. He refers to copyeditors as 'ideal readers' (Jeyamohan 2018)[1]. Authors know their subject, especially in academic publishing, where most authors are highly accomplished academicians and researchers. However, their very knowledge often affects their judgement because they fail to perceive any gaps in the discussion – gaps filled by the authors' cognitive bias and therefore invisible to them. Authors are

1 Jeyamohan is a well-known South Indian writer who writes in Tamil and Malayalam. *Vishnupuram* and *Venmurasu* are his masterpieces. *Venmurasu*, a re-creation of the epic *Mahabharata*, is hailed as the longest novel written ever. Jeyamohan refused to accept the Padma Shri Award from the Government of India (2016) on the grounds of preserving his integrity. A regular blogger, he once wrote about the role of copyediting in Tamil writing and explained the process succinctly. If you can read Tamil, you will love this piece: www.jeyamohan.in/106575/

weighed down by their existing knowledge, which makes it difficult for them to identify any inadequacies in their writing. This is what we call the 'curse of knowledge'. In these circumstances, it is usually the copyeditor who, donning the hat of the ideal reader, rightly identifies the kinks in the text. This makes copyediting indispensable to the writing process. The copyeditor thus becomes, in Jeyamohan's words, the ideal reader – ideal because a copyeditor knows what the author wants to convey and ensures that the written text communicates that thought.

The copyeditor comprehends the implied meaning, grasps the author's implicit message, identifies blocks of text that fail to deliver the author's thoughts intelligibly, and proposes ways in which the author can improve the text to communicate the message more clearly. The copyeditor possesses not just the ability to follow the author's stream of thought but also the adeptness to read between the lines; in other words, the copyeditor reads what is conveyed in the lines and what is conveyed between the lines.

WHAT IS THE ULTIMATE GOAL OF A COPYEDITOR?

What then is the ultimate goal of a copyeditor? It is to ensure that the reader clearly understands the written text. A text that is readable flows smoothly, ensuring that the reader follows the author's line of thought without any difficulties and comprehends the author's ideas easily. The importance of readability has been reiterated by many. For example, Steven Allen (n.d.) stresses that "a writer's style should not place obstacles between his ideas and the minds of his readers"; Mathew Arnold echoed these thoughts when he said to G W E Russell, his biographer: "Have something to say, and say it as clearly as you can. That is the only secret of style" (Russell 1904). Sometimes readability may suffer because of convoluted text, ambiguous sentences, circumlocution, error-ridden syntax, excessive use of jargon, garden-path sentences[2], and other basic errors. The copyeditor removes such obstacles and errors and enhances the clarity of the text.

WHO BECOMES A GREAT COPYEDITOR?

Let us turn our attention to the question, What coveted traits does a copyeditor possess?

There is no textbook definition of the traits of a copyeditor. Although many people may add or substitute a few other qualities, four qualities form the basic requirements for one to be a copyeditor: proficiency in grammar, a flair for reading, an eye for detail, and inquisitiveness (Shanmugam 2015).

Proficiency in grammar is a primary requirement to be a good copyeditor. Grammar rules are, in general, not complex and often have exceptions. As Noam Chomsky (1970) puts it, "Language is a process of free creation; its laws and principles are fixed, but the manner in which the principles of generation are used is free and infinitely varied." Copyeditors must possess not only a sound knowledge of the rules and exceptions of grammar but also the profound awareness that the context largely determines the appropriate syntax or usage. In short, copyediting is nothing but the application of common sense.

The second trait that confers an added advantage to a copyeditor is a flair for reading. If we may take the liberty to tweak Francis Bacon's words, reading maketh a full copyeditor (originally "reading maketh a full man"). Being a voracious reader nurtures the copyeditor's innate ability to assess the writer's style, judge the tone, and follow the flow of thought.

Thirdly, eye for detail. Copyeditors must be able to identify

2 The American Psychological Association's *Dictionary of Psychology* defines a garden-path sentence as "a sentence in which structural cues, lexical ambiguity, or a combination of both mislead the reader or listener into an incorrect interpretation until a disambiguating cue appears later in the sentence" (APA 2015).

inconsistencies or lapses commonly overlooked by others. Lastly, copyeditors must be inquisitive. Proficiency in grammar and wide reading often help copyeditors to spot awkward text. Once they identify such a patch of text, encouraged by their inquisitiveness, copyeditors seek answers to remove the oddity. All these qualities are not acquired in a day: it takes years of earnest and persistent practice to become an acclaimed copyeditor.

WHO IS AN L3 EDITOR?

There are many levels of intervention in copyediting as determined by the author who seeks the help of a copyeditor. Most typesetting companies in India, the hub of world's academic publishing services, define three levels of copyediting.

In Level 1 editing, generally called light editing or, colloquially, L1 editing, the copyeditor ensures consistency of mechanical aspects that include spelling, capitalization, punctuation, abbreviations, and hyphenation. As you would have guessed, manuscripts that require L1 editing are written by authors who have a good command over their subject and the language. The copyeditor is often provided with style sheets that carry a list of preferences of the publishing house in matters of spelling, capitalization, hyphenation, etc.

In Level 2 editing, also known as standard editing or L2 editing, besides addressing the mechanical aspects, the copyeditor points out sentences that seem verbose or convoluted. The level of intervention in terms of rewording/rewriting text is higher in L2 editing.

Level 3 editing, commonly referred to as substantive editing in international parlance and colloquially as L3 editing, is often regarded as niche or elite editing. Here, in addition to fixing grammatical and syntax errors, the copyeditor rewrites ambiguous sentences to improve clarity. An L3 editor also judges the purpose of the text and assesses whether the language and tone are appropriate for target readers. Besides checking the sense and flow of the text, the L3 editor removes digressions and restructures paragraphs to enhance coherence. A natural elevation for a copyeditor is to become a so-called L3 editor.

What makes one an L3 editor?

Besides the four characteristics mentioned earlier that make a copyeditor, yet another significant trait distinguishes an L3 editor from others: an L3 editor is a lifelong learner. On a lighter note, L3 can stand for lifelong learning. After all, "The illiterates of the future are not those who can't read or write but those who cannot learn, unlearn, and relearn".[3] An L3 editor follows this dictum: language is dynamic and eternally evolving, and so must the L3 editor.

SO, ARE YOU READY TO BECOME A COPYEDITOR?

We live in the information age. Never before in the annals of history has humankind enjoyed such boundless access to information. While the whole world bears the yoke of this information overload, one wonders who the gatekeepers of this information are. The onus is on many, and the copyeditor is one of them because the copyeditor strives to ensure that knowledge is relayed flawlessly.

REFERENCES

APA. 2015. *APA Dictionary of Psychology*, 2nd edn, pp. 447–448. Washington, DC: American Psychological Association. 1204 pp.

Butcher J, Drake C, and Leach M. 2006. *Butcher's Copy-Editing: the Cambridge handbook for editors, copy-editors and proofreaders*, 3rd edn. Cambridge, UK: Cambridge University Press. 544 pp.

3 This quote is widely attributed to Alvin Toffler (1971), but these words were said by Psychologist Herbert Gerjuoy of the Human Resources Research Organization and quoted by Toffler. You may read more here: https://flexnib.com/2013/07/03/that-alvin-toffler-quotation/

Chomsky N. 1970. *For Reasons of State*, p. 402. New York: Pantheon Books. 440 pp.

Einsohn A and Schwartz M. 2019. *The Copyeditor's Handbook: a guide for book publishing and corporate communications*, 4th edn. Berkeley: University of California Press. 584 pp.

Jeyamohan. 2018. https://www.jeyamohan.in/106575/

Russell G W E. 1904. *Matthew Arnold*. New York: Scribner.

Shanmugam M. 2015. https://tinyurl.com/blogcopyeditor

Toffler A. 1971. *Future Shock*. New York: Bantam Books.

Murugaraj Shanmugam (murugaraj@tholga.com) is the founder-director of Tholga Publishing Services, which he established after working for 18 years with major typesetting companies in India, setting up and managing their copyediting teams. He specializes in academic editing; teaches copyediting through Editor's Essentials (https://editorsessentials.com), the training arm of Tholga Publishing Services; and mentors copyeditors. As an active member of the Indian Copyeditors Forum, he has delivered many webinars on language and Microsoft Word for editors.

CHAPTER 2

Learning Copyediting: An Overview

Venkataraman Anantharaman

This chapter provides an overview of the main things you have to learn to become a copyeditor.

COPYEDITING AS A PROFESSION AND THE NEED FOR TRAINING AND MENTORING

There are many different professions in the world, each requiring a different timeline for getting trained in the profession.

Suppose you want to learn gardening. First, you will have to consider how small or big a place you have and what you can grow there. Having known that (at least in a general way), you will have to prepare the soil for growing what you want to grow. And this is where you get your hands dirty, bruised, and even put up with foul smell. Then you sow what you want to grow and take care of it every day. After a certain time (depending on what you are growing), you will see the fruit of your efforts.

In the same way, we have to look at what copyediting is and what we have to do to learn the art. This is like that first step of knowing what land you have and what you can grow there.

Reading habit

Reading, writing, and editing are related skills and so we can first look at them together. Do you have a reading habit? Without a good reading habit, it might not be worthwhile attempting to become a copyeditor. Why? Being a copyeditor implies a lifelong learning career (along with the editing you do to earn a living); off and on, you will have to read and understand something completely new (something related to what you are editing). It simply means that when you come across a problem, you read up something about it till you find a solution (and do it quickly), and then continue with your copyediting. This will happen day in and day out, long after you have learnt copyediting. So, do you have a reading habit? Are you determined to cultivate that habit – to make it part and parcel of your life?

Physical and mental actions

Physical actions can often be learnt more quickly than mental actions. You may be able to learn driving in about 10–15 days (even with a short practice every day). But you need a longer time to learn (say) Microsoft Excel, as you will have to learn how Excel as a program works in general, its phenomenal features as a number-crunching and spreadsheet program, and the ways by which you can combine its features to do something complex, and how you can use automation to do things quickly and consistently. The reason why you need more time to learn Excel – remember, this is just an example – is that you will need some time to learn and understand a concept, some more time to learn another concept, yet more time to combine these concepts, and so on. So, the learning here is gradual, as each aspect must be grasped before taking up the next one.

When we analyse all the actions we do, we'll find that thinking – and thinking clearly – and communicating clearly in any language are very complex actions. I'll give you a practical example.

We all know that learning medicine (and becoming a doctor) takes a long time, and becoming a surgeon takes a still longer time.

Performing surgery is also a complex action – a surgeon has assistants to help during the process – and more so as the surgery is performed on a living being. Even then, despite its complexity, scientists have managed to conduct successful surgeries using robots – without human intervention. This has been possible because surgery involves physical actions based on available data. On the other hand, it has still not been possible to automate writing[1] and editing, as this involves perception, understanding, analysis, reasoning, evaluation, and decision-making, which are all purely human characteristics. No matter how much we standardize our training methods, every individual will have to go through these steps in one's own mind. Thinking is what makes us different from (and superior to) any other creature on this planet, and each one thinks differently (even with guided thinking). And if we can replace that aspect, the planet will not need human beings, and human beings as a race will be on its way to extinction.

"Reading maketh a full man, conference a ready man, and writing an exact man", said Francis Bacon, about 400 years ago. And that statement will be valid forever. It takes a long time to write precisely – and it naturally takes a long time to edit precisely.

A writer is concerned with expressing one's thoughts, and an editor is concerned with polishing that content to make it enjoyable. Writers and editors share the same base in the sense that both have to master the craft of writing.

Training and mentoring

No matter how good you were in grammar in your school and college days, you will still need training to understand copyediting as a profession. You will need 3–5 years of training, followed (parallelly)

1 The introduction of ChatGPT in November 2022 has raised several questions as to what artificial intelligence (and machines) can and cannot do. It can definitely help in consolidation of information, possibly with some associated hardships for humanity at large.

by *learning on the job* under a mentor, to achieve a decent level of competency. If you have a good reading habit, it can help in minimizing some of the practical difficulties in the learning process.

So, the first thing is to *be aware of the need for training and learning under a mentor and the timelines involved.*

BASIC SKILLS USED IN ROUTINE COPYEDITING

Copyediting is a tricky profession: it requires an uncanny concentration, far beyond what an average person is capable of. So, is the copyeditor a specially gifted person? Not necessarily. But some are lucky enough to get the right kind of training at the very beginning, and that helps them to progress steadily in their career.

If you are editing fiction, you may not have headings and subheadings, figures, tables, and footnotes. But you will encounter almost all of these if you're editing non-fiction. If you are editing academic manuscripts, you will have references (brief citations in the text as well as the details of each provided in the form of a list at the end of the document). You may also have hundreds of scientific conventions within the main text of the document.

One aim of copyediting is to help the typesetter format the document correctly, whatever be the final device or physical form in which it may be read. A simple wedding invitation will have just a few lines of text and the typesetter may be able to set it correctly within your desired card size and give you what is called a proof for you to see how the final presentation will look like (and you may even make some corrections to it to satisfy your own ideas of how the card should be). But an academic document will have many fixed and movable elements, most of which may not be clear to the typesetter. So, the first task of a copyeditor is markup – marking up the manuscript or identifying all the elements for the typesetter.

Books and journals have a preconceived design laid out in the form of typesetting specifications. When the typesetter applies the specifications to each of the elements identified by the copyeditor, we will have a typeset page.

Identifying manuscript elements – about 20–30 elements in journals to even 200 or more elements in complex books – is a comparatively simple task that a copyeditor can learn quickly (a few days to a fortnight). But understanding the conventions relating to handling numbers and associated elements as well as the myriad scientific conventions present in a manuscript may require a much longer time. Similarly, learning to style reference citations and a list of references per specific and detailed preferences will also take a long time.

It is not that learning number-related preferences, scientific conventions, and reference-style preferences are difficult. Rather, it is here that you will see the difficulty associated with the copyediting process. Often, you will know what to do, but you will miss things repeatedly, which will make you understand how poor human focus is in general. When you continue to work on these repeatedly, you will also learn to improve and increase your attention span and gradually be able to attend to these things to near perfection.

Understanding grammar and connecting it to the (often highly technical) content you read, understanding the intent of the writer, the style of writing, power of expression, and the like are things that will require a still longer time. And it is here that you will appreciate how your earlier practice with numbers, scientific conventions, and reference styling have all helped to prepare you for the longer attention span, analysis, and decision-making you will so desperately need while editing content.

To summarize, we can say that in copyediting we'll use the following skills:

- simple formatting skills (for which some computer knowledge may be necessary)
- some learning and focusing skills that basically improve our attention span more and more

- all our grammar skills (which we will have to learn and hone)
- analytical and decision-making skills

LEARNING WINDOWS AND MICROSOFT WORD SHORTCUTS

Nowadays, almost all college students are familiar with PCs, Macs, and laptops. But rarely does anyone learn to use a computer professionally while in college.

Most editing is done in Microsoft Word, although Google Docs, LibreOffice, and TeX may also be used by some. Microsoft Word has certain important features (in addition to its user interface) that make it a favourite for editors:

- A phenomenal suite of keyboard shortcuts to perform your routine tasks efficiently
- Ability to track changes/revisions made to the original document
- Facility to add comments (to help cowriters, for example, indicate perspectives on any thought/sentence to each other)
- Document formatting using Word Styles
- Facility to use macros to ensure consistency and speed up complex tasks
- Background XML support, which is quite important in today's digital world

Microsoft Word is such an efficient word-processing program that even Mac users use Word for Mac for their professional editing. If you are entering the editing profession, keep in mind, however, that Word works best in its native Windows platform.

For this reason, it becomes important to learn how to use Word efficiently. Windows and Word shortcuts are the very first things you should learn as soon as you join the editing profession, perhaps within the first 1–3 months.

FORMATTING ASPECTS OF COPYEDITING

Figure 2.1 shows a division of copyediting into markup and language editing. This is purely for convenience; the former relates to certain mechanical aspects of copyediting and the latter relates to tougher analytical aspects. Copyediting is best done by a single person (and not done by two or three persons, each one doing some part of it, as is done in many companies in India).

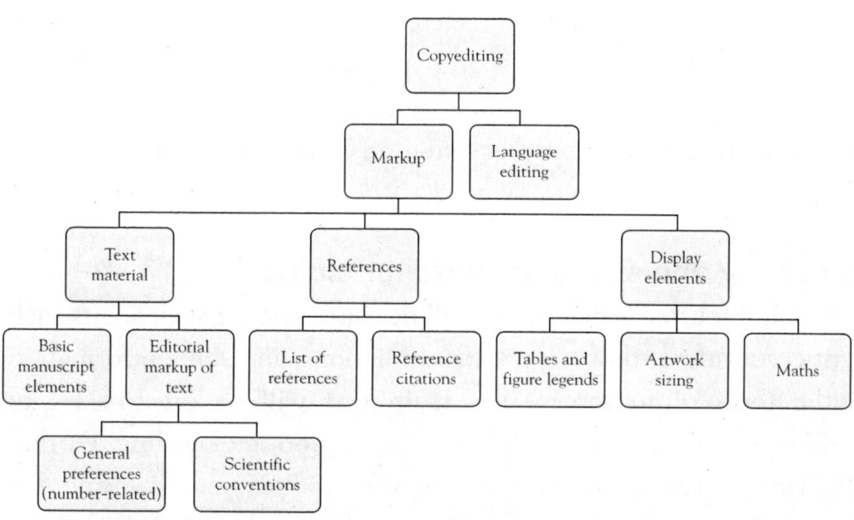

Figure 2.1 Breakdown of markup into understandable components. (Reproduced from The Art of Copyediting website: https://theartofcopyediting.com/)

Markup relates to formatting and the editorial-style aspects of the publication process. Every scientific document can be broken down into main text, display elements, and a list of references at the end.

References

The references in a document are made up of a brief citation in the text and an expanded version in the list of references. To understand references, you must, however, start with the list of references and then learn about reference citations. A note of caution would be in order here. Theoretically, it may be difficult to comprehend the complex activity called styling the list of references; attending to reference citations may seem comparatively easier. In practice, however, reference styling will become clearer and easier as you work on more and more manuscripts. But setting right reference citations, particularly when they are not given per style – and there are many reasons why this may happen – will test your understanding and patience! Then you'll know that attending to reference citations is one of the most exacting tasks in copyediting.

Identifying and styling manuscript elements

In a typical journal article, there will be some title-page elements such as title, subtitle, author names and affiliations, and some information in the form of footnotes. The main text will be organized into sections and subsections, each having an appropriate heading. Further delineation may be in the form of lists, quoted material, and the like. Books may have learning objectives, boxed elements (sometimes even with headings and subheadings), chapter summaries, and chapter review questions. All these will have to be formatted consistently in any publication.

Editorial markup of text

Within the main text, we may have a thousand tiny things that may have to be set according to publication-specific preferences or according to scientific conventions prevailing in the field of science the document relates to. A huge chunk of the former is mechanical in nature and may be set right by an understanding of the principles and preferences relating to the handling of numbers in a document. Scientific conventions may or may not be associated with numbers, but these too are simple mechanical aspects. All these can be handled efficiently (by Find and Replace actions) when some fundamental principles are understood.

Markup of maths

Maths is a specialized subset of scientific conventions (involving both in-line and display maths), and many things can go wrong with the typesetting of a maths manuscript. Learning to mark up a maths manuscript will be a separate area of learning if one deals with academic content.

Tables and figure legends

Display elements are often in the form of tables and figures, which have captions and legends respectively. Artwork-sizing (earlier handled as part of copyediting) is now handled almost entirely by a separate graphics team. Nevertheless, some rare situations do occur where a copyeditor may advise the typesetter on the positioning of some artwork. Training programmes may discuss tables and figure legends separately or discuss them together as a group.

Learning formatting first

If you join a company and are lucky enough to get into journal editing, you may have the time to learn all the above (often by helping somebody) before getting into serious editing of content. But some may not be lucky enough. If you are put into book editing straightaway, you may be forced to start looking at content very early, and you may be expected to learn the formatting aspects side by side and at a much quicker pace (which, to put it straight, can be tough).

ANALYTICAL ASPECTS OF COPYEDITING

In the West, where copyediting first evolved as a profession, editing simply meant polishing the content – because that is how it first started. Formatting aspects (discussed in the earlier section) became part of copyediting only as part of interactions between editing and typesetting – by observation of typeset pages.

So editing as such implies understanding of content (at least to the level necessary for editing) and polishing the expression of content. This is an analytical process that involves a high level of focus.

As mentioned earlier, both writers and editors have to master the craft of writing. But there is a difference: writers may not be editors, but an editor must master the craft of writing. Otherwise, how will he or she correct grammatical mistakes or polish somebody else's writing? And imagine doing that on a scholarly manuscript!

So a copyeditor has to master some important aspects of the writing process, which are listed below:

- Some of the most basic principles involved in any type of writing (apostrophe use, subject–verb agreement, organizing one's thoughts and sentences into paragraphs and sections, using punctuation marks correctly, knowing how to punctuate simple, compound, and complex sentences, using parallel construction for forceful expression)
- The use of commas (the most misused among punctuation marks)
- Verbs, tenses, and voice – and the grammar associated with all these
- Article use (an important area, more so because some languages have articles and some don't, and the English language also has its own quirky preferences)
- The use of hyphens and en dashes (a complex area by itself and is therefore better learnt after the earlier topics have been understood to a good extent)

Once these have been learnt, they have to be practised till one feels confident about them. It is only after this protracted practice that one should learn under a mentor to iron out the remaining kinks in the understanding.

These are the basics. Once a person becomes a completely independent editor, he or she will be engaged in a lifelong learning process, basically connected with word usage.

UNDERSTANDING COPYEDITING AS PART OF THE PUBLISHING WORKFLOW

Once you start getting into the thick of work, you will learn that your work is closely connected with typesetting, no matter what the final reading platform may be. And most often, you may use Microsoft Word for your work. But even here, in academic work, each company may use a different workflow. Some may use in-line codes for identification of manuscript elements, some may use Word Styles, and some may want you to edit on XML files. In newspaper and magazine type of work, the editing may be done in typically laid-out pages. In school-book type of work, the content and the illustrations may evolve with the progression of the work.

Just as you grow in your knowledge of copyediting, you must also grow in your understanding of the overall production process, and perhaps gain an overview of the entire publishing process. It is not necessary to know these in depth, but an overall idea will be helpful as you move forward in your career.

FINAL THOUGHTS

Here's a summary of what you can do:

- Take some solid training in copyediting and practise diligently for some time.

- Learn how to use Microsoft Word effectively. Start with Windows and Word shortcuts and then learn to take advantage of the power of Word styles and templates. Finally, learn how to use Word macros to ensure consistency as well as to automate repeated tasks.
- Seek out a mentor who is willing to review your work and give you feedback.
- Become a member of some international forums after a year or two. Read and observe the discussions that happen there. Can you follow the questions that people ask in these forums? How good is your knowledge? Can you answer the questions asked by other editors in these forums? (We're not talking about geographical or culture-specific expressions, but about general written English.)
- Plan to go for an editorial certification about five years after you begin working in the field.

These will give you some idea of where you stand and whether you can really edit at an international level (and perhaps become part of an international community of copyeditors).

Dr Venkataraman Anantharaman is the founder of The Art of Copyediting.
After obtaining a PhD in clinical biochemistry, he decided to explore the writing/editing aspects of science, and has been at it for about 28 years now. He offers copyediting training to companies as well as individuals.
Global site: https://theartofcopyediting.com/
Indian site: https://www.theartofcopyediting.com/ri-home-page

CHAPTER 3

Where to Look for Work as a Copyeditor

Venkatesh Krishnamoorthy and Vivek Kumar

In an incisive account of writing and his life, *On Writing: a memoir of the craft*, the legendary storyteller and author Stephen King (2001) declares, "[T]o write is human, to edit is divine." Copyeditors are a special breed of professionals whose niche is their linguistic skills and yet, most copyeditors in India would confess that they found their first copyediting job not by choice but by accident. Just as journalists are required to have a nose for news, copyeditors are prized for their ability to spot errors and for an eye for detail. Often, people become copyeditors when they, because of their language skills, are asked to check a piece of writing (usually to correct grammar) by their friends, family members, or colleagues – without realizing that such work can provide professional employment.

A professional copyeditor remains an unknown entity outside of publishing or news organizations in India although copyeditors are employed in a host of organizations in domains other than publishing and the mass media. Among fresh graduates, postgraduates, or even those who have completed a PhD, awareness of copyediting as a profession is abysmally low despite the fact that employment opportunities for copyeditors opened up on a large scale as a result of India becoming a hub of publishing services for academic publishers.

In the United States and the United Kingdom – countries with a very high concentration of copyeditors – a few universities, other organizations, and copyediting associations offer courses on copyediting and publishing that help land jobs. In India, such training is largely offered in-house once you join an organization as a copyeditor and it takes some years of toiling in the trenches to gain expertise.

FINDING A COPYEDITING JOB

Often, being appreciated for their good command of English has given many potential copyeditors the confidence to apply for the job. The ideal educational qualification for becoming a copyeditor is a master's degree, but some organizations may also be inclined to recruit fresh graduates with a degree in English, science, history, or any discipline in the humanities.

Newspapers are a valuable resource for finding a job as a copyeditor because in India, potential employers often advertise in leading English dailies. You could send in your résumé and await a response. A few organizations may prefer to conduct walk-in interviews and usually conduct a short test, which typically tests your ability to identify errors in a piece of text or in a number of unrelated sentences and may include a short writing assignment.

Many editors have found their first copyediting jobs through newspaper advertisements or have been referred to by friends and sometimes by their professors or family members. Word-of-mouth referrals are a very common way to find copyediting jobs, especially in Delhi, a city with many organizations looking for copyeditors. It is not uncommon to be recommended by someone with whom you have no direct connection, by a friend's friend for example.

If you live far away, you may also be asked to take a test and send it through email. If you clear the test, you may be interviewed online (through Zoom, Google Meet, etc.), and the employer could encourage you to work remotely after providing some training, online or in person or a combination of both, lasting a few days or spread over a few months. Further learning then happens on the job.

Ujwala Vaidyanathan, Senior Manager at Newgen Knowledge Works, a knowledge-process outsourcing (KPO) organization, elaborates on the process of testing new copyeditors:

> Copyediting tests involve correcting simple grammatical errors including subject–verb disagreement, tense mismatch, and typos. There is also an essay to be written. On successful completion of these tests, candidates are given a copyediting test, which tests their knowledge of idioms and phrases, eye for detail, consistency checking, fact-checking, notes and reference editing, etc.

She adds that a newbie copyeditor should "show the right attitude to learning". On what it takes to complete training, she observes, "Openness to learning and building on lessons learned with every project ensure that training is successful." She stresses the importance of timeliness and quality consciousness as important attributes of a copyeditor.

Visalakshy Loganathan, who runs Onpaper Publishing, which provides alt-text writing services, says, "An ideal candidate should possess excellent English-language skills, good analytical skills, and problem-solving skills, and has to be sensitive to the needs of visually impaired people."

You could also find job postings in online job portals such as Naukri.com or Indeed.com although only a few postings are for copyeditors; these portals are usually filled with jobs related to IT (information technology).

Even if you are not out of college yet, you could land a copyediting job through on-campus recruitment. Many organizations throng the campuses, looking for potential copyeditors among postgraduates or even those on the verge of completing their PhD.

Your presence on social media (Facebook, Twitter, LinkedIn, etc.) may also lead you to opportunities in copyediting. Your profile on LinkedIn (creating one is a good idea if you already do not have one) may interest a potential employer. Some opportunities could also arise from your activity on Facebook and Twitter. Because copyediting is sought by individuals, social media might also lead you to unknown or surprising finds, which may eventually pull you into copyediting: if you find someone on social media calling for copyeditors, you would want to grab the opportunity.

College students and others looking for jobs may get placed as interns in some organizations willing to bet on their skills and provide them with some incentive (training and money).

WHO NEEDS COPYEDITORS?

It is commonly known that publishers employ copyeditors. Opportunities for copyeditors are also aplenty in organizations in which any form of writing of some length and formality is undertaken or worked upon. Here are some avenues largely in academic and scholarly publishing.

Traditional book publishers

An internship (read 'a foot in the door') with a traditional book publishing company (Penguin Random House, Rupa, Roli Books, Oxford University Press, HarperCollins, Hachette, and Bloomsbury are some names that readily come to mind) is what a literature graduate ideally looks for, although such opportunities are not many (see Table 3.1). Textbook publishers, academic publishers, and trade publishers are the three main types of traditional publishers in descending order of size.

Table 3.1 Companies providing internship opportunities[a]

No.	Entity offering internship and point of contact	Place	Internship area
1	Amnet ContentSource recruitment@theenerjigroup.com	Chennai	Editorial
2	Newgen KnowledgeWorks Subhash subhashp@newgen.co	Chennai	Printing
3	Tara Books https://tarabooks.com/	Chennai	All aspects of publishing
4	Tholga Publishing Services Murugaraj Shanmugam murugaraj@tholga.com	Chennai	Copyediting
5	The Browser Pankaj Singh pankaj@99beagles.com	Chandigarh	Editorial, sales and marketing
6	Blue Rose Publishers https://bluerosepublishers.com/	Delhi	Publishing
7	Disha Publishing Deepak Agarwal hr@aiets.co.in	Delhi	Editorial
8	Grapevine India https://grapevineindia.com	Delhi	Editing and publishing
9	Manjul Publishing House Rashmi Menon rashmi@amaryllis.co.in	Delhi	Editorial, online (over the phone); selection is based on a test
10	Oakbridge Publishing Bhupendra Yadav bhupendra.y@oakbridge.in	Delhi	

Table 3.1 Companies providing internship opportunities[a] (*continued*)

No.	Entity offering internship and point of contact	Place	Internship area
11	Orange Education https://www.orangeeducation.in	Delhi	
12	Readomania Indrani Ganguly indrani.ganguly@readomania.com	Delhi	Marketing and social media
13	Rupa Publications https://rupapublications.co.in	Delhi	Copyediting
14	Vitasta Publishing Renu Kaul Verma renukverma@vitastapublishing.com	Delhi	Editorial, content and digital marketing/sales
15	Hachette India[b] jobs@hachetteindia.com	Gurgaon	Editorial, PR, events, marketing
16	Penguin Random House	Gurgaon	All aspects of publishing
17	Siyahi (https://siyahi.in/) Mita Kapur mita.kapur@gmail.com	Jaipur	All aspects of publishing
18	Oxford University Press India https://india.oup.com/	Noida	Publishing
19	S Chand Manisha Bharti mbharti1@schandpublishing.com	Noida	Editorial
20	Vikas Publishing https://www.vikaspublishing.com/	Noida	

Table 3.1 Companies providing internship opportunities[a] (*continued*)

No.	Entity offering internship and point of contact	Place	Internship area
21	Aarahan Publishers Nirja Sharma support@aarahanpublishers.com	Pune	Editorial and publishing
22	TechKnowledge Publications https://techknowledgebooks.com/	Pune	Editing of pharmaceutical books
23	Authors Upfront Manish Purohit manish@authorsupfront.com	Pune or Mumbai	Author coordination

[a] Internship duration ranges from 1 month to 1 year.
[b] Use subject line 'Internship'.

Self-publishers

Self-publishing has come up in a big way in the last few years, so much so that even companies such as Amnet have started offering such services (www.Buuks.com) to authors. Newgen, in fact, has three imprints (Indus, Trove, and 16Leaves). Other self-publishing companies include Notion Press and Pothi.com (https://pothi.com/), and all of them employ both full-time in-house editors and freelance editors.

Independent publishers

Independent publishers are small but often publish brilliant work. Some of the names in this category are Pickle Yolk Books, Seagull Books, and Copper Coin.

Start-ups

The digital ecosystem has also thrown the doors open to start-ups in publishing. Some of the names in this category are www.nextpub.co.in, https://skillmonde.com/, and https://www.letsauthor.com/

Media houses

Those with a diploma in journalism can safely rely on campus placement or being absorbed in a media house that ran the journalism school they attended (for more details, see Chapter 8, 'Copyediting for newspapers and magazines' by Reena Singh).

KPO organizations: editing peer-reviewed work

A science graduate can also try the various KPO organizations (Aptara, Thomson Digital, Straive, etc.) in cities such as Bengaluru, Chennai, Dehra Dun, Delhi, Mumbai, Noida, Puducherry, and Pune. These organizations advertise their vacancies in newspapers, on LinkedIn, and also in the ICF Jobs Database (https://tinyurl.com/icfdatabase) and jobs-related WhatsApp groups that are part of the Indian Copyeditors Forum.

An editing office provides the best environment for newcomers to learn on the job because they get access not only to specialized dictionaries, other reference books, software packages, and so on but also to senior copyeditors who can review the newcomers' work. Exposure to a variety of copyediting jobs – and of authors – is also much greater if the firm caters to many clients. The manuscripts you edit would mostly be peer-reviewed books and journal articles. Therefore, knowledge of the subject does not matter as much as it would if you were working on material that has not been peer reviewed (see the section 'On your own: choosing the path less travelled' later in this chapter).

Post the COVID-19 pandemic, things are slightly different because most companies have begun to offer the work-from-home option to their employees, which confines interaction among them only to the online mode. Is it possible to learn on the job online? We know of at least two companies – Editor's Essentials (https://editorsessentials.com) and The Art of Copyediting (https://www.theartofcopyediting.com/ri-home-page) – that have started offering on-the-job office experience online. They offer a hybrid model comprising recorded and live classes, practice material, mentorship, and even the possibility of working as an intern (offered only by Editor's Essentials) once the training is complete.

Unconventional employers

Some of the unconventional and less-known places that employ editors are institutions (colleges and universities), non-governmental organizations (NGOs), translation bureaus, book cafés, agencies of the central government (National Book Trust and Sahitya Akademi), training institutes, and booksellers.

Surit Das, an independent consultant specializing in grey literature (reports, issue briefs, grant proposals, etc.) and working mainly with the development sector, academics, and research organizations, elaborates on opportunities for copyeditors outside the traditional avenues: "The banking, financial services, and insurance (BFSI) industry, and the consulting industry, employs quite a few editors, but few jobs are advertised." Specialist knowledge of the domain is needed to get a job in this sector.

Surit goes on to say:

> Business research and analytics is another domain. A few editors switch from publishing or publishing services to such niches but most start their careers in publishing. Jobs are typically in-house, but a few firms now use the hybrid model. Jobs are full time; part-time or freelance work is not available.

He adds that a few jobs are available in the development sector with NGOs, international NGOs (INGOs), quasi-NGOs (QUANGOs), and multilateral organizations.

> Almost all opportunities are ad hoc and contractual. The organizations look for individual freelance editors at times. People with experience look for RFPs (request for proposals) or RFQs (request for quotes) at sites such as devnetjobs.org and at sites that post jobs advertised online by organizations in the UN system. Consulting firms in the development sector, too, operate the same way.

Your operating style for this kind of editing differs from that for the traditional publishing workflow. Surit says, "To develop the content, the editor must understand the organization's purpose for conducting the exercise." He further adds:

> Much of the content is specialized and written in the appropriate argot, and it is not possible for anyone to know it all, so fundamental literacy and numeracy are critical, as is the sense of knowing when to search online and when to ask the client for clarification. An understanding of the content and audience is useful.

ON YOUR OWN: CHOOSING THE PATH LESS TRAVELLED

After a few years of working with a publisher, a publishing service provider (also called a KPO), a research organization, or any other organization that undertakes copyediting, a copyeditor can choose to become a freelancer. Becoming a freelance copyeditor without formal training or knowing the job is not impossible, provided the organization that agrees to take you on as a freelancer is willing to train you (see the following sections).

Working with material that has not been peer reviewed

A few organizations sometimes take on as freelance copyeditors those with no prior editing experience. For years, Cactus Communications and Enago have been good starting points for such editors. The work offered comprises manuscripts of research papers mostly by authors from Asian countries or other countries with English as a second language who need help to get published in their target journals – which are almost always English-language journals. The manuscripts are yet to undergo peer review, which happens only after the manuscript is submitted to a journal for possible publication – and that too only if the journal considers it good enough to be sent out for peer review in the first place. Therefore, you need top-notch language skills first to decipher what the authors want to say and then to render it in standard and clear English. Because the authors often think in their native language and then translate their thoughts into English, some knowledge of the subject of the manuscript proves to be of considerable help.

Lekshmi Dinachandran, who joined Cactus as a freelance copyeditor, recalls her experience:

> Cactus offered a well-structured training that was administered rather informally. I was among the first to be trained over Skype. The training required model assignments to be submitted on a deadline, and regular feedback sessions were conducted by the trainer.

Asked which part of the training was valuable to her, Lekshmi responds:

> The detailed feedback given by the trainer and the curated content on the Cactus Knowledge Base. The feedback helped identify patterns in my editing style, whereas the knowledge base ensured that I did not have to look elsewhere. I did, however, realize later that I had aligned my editing style too closely to the Cactus procedure and found it a

> bit difficult to adapt to other clients and their demands. Therefore, I had to re-educate myself, but I believe the foundation of my work process was laid at Cactus.

Lekshmi adds that as a result of this training, she "developed an eye for glaring and common mistakes, a good understanding of academic style, and, most important, time management."

Working with independent authors

One can also work with independent authors (researchers and writers of fiction or non-fiction) seeking to get their articles published or to increase the chances of their book-length manuscripts being accepted by a traditional book publisher by submitting a quality manuscript. Even those looking to self-publish need an editor. But how do these people find you? Get a shop front (a website) and market your services both online and offline. Contact universities. Join writers' or readers' groups.

Working with editors operating an editing business

Experienced editors with an entrepreneurial spirit often set up their own teams and they take on experienced editors as well as freshers as team members. Quite a few members of the ICF – Shweta Bharti Dayal of Scribblers & Scribes, Murugaraj Shanmugam (www.tholga.com), Chitralekha Manohar (www.thecleancopy.com), and Visalakshy Loganathan (http://onpaperpublishing.com/), to mention a few – work as entrepreneurs, and you can check with them how you can join their editing or alt-text teams. This can also be a good avenue to both learn (on the job) and earn. You might learn more in a small team because chances of one-to-one interaction, feedback, and mentorship are more in a small team. You also get to learn a lot of things other than editing, such as how to give feedback to authors, how to respond to feedback from authors and from your supervisors, how to interact with clients, and how to interact with your team members offline and online.

Working in the international market

One of the many ways to explore freelance options worldwide is to join such editing associations as the Editorial Freelancers Association (https://www.the-efa.org), the European Association of Science Editors (https://ease.org.uk), which now has an India chapter, ACES: the Society for Editing (https://aceseditors.org), and the Chartered Institute of Editing and Proofreading (https://www.ciep.uk). A membership provides you with access to a job board, a chance to interact with fellow members, enrol in courses, and buy books and other relevant materials at a discount. You can also attend events (webinars, workshops, meetings, conferences, etc.) in person or online. You can even work from anywhere and be a digital nomad.

CONCLUSION

Copyediting is a challenging but an exciting profession. Many copyeditors who initially got into copyediting either did not intend to stay long or thought of it as a stopgap arrangement until they found a better job. But they stayed on to love their jobs and were amazed at its potential to provide not only their daily bread but also a lifetime skill they can depend on without an expiry date. The initial days as a copyeditor are not only lively but also energizing. You may often receive appreciation for doing a good job, which will pave the way for your future growth. Acquiring copyediting skills would stand you in good stead, and opportunities would open up as you go along.

PREPARING TO BE A COPYEDITOR

Here are some tips from a few experienced copyeditors to help you navigate the initial phases of your life as a copyeditor and to succeed.

Searching for copyediting jobs

Anupam Chaudhury, who was a managing editor at Oxford University Press before moving to freelancing, emphasizes excellent knowledge of English grammar, above-average language skills including writing and speaking, and professional demeanour as important for a new copyeditor. He also suggests some ways of searching for copyediting jobs.

- Responding to advertisements in newspapers and online platforms such as LinkedIn and Naukri
- Connecting with HR professionals and consultants who represent publishing houses
- Networking with professionals who already work in publishing houses (through LinkedIn)
- Cold-calling and directly applying to publishing houses (could also work for internships)
- Becoming members of forums and associations such as the Indian Copyeditors Forum (sometimes publishers check these forums when looking for editors)
- Doing courses from established organizations such as the Seagull School of Publishing and the National Book Trust, because sometimes publishers go to these institutes for placements.

What copyediting demands

Copyediting is a demanding job. Chitralekha Manohar, the founding editor of The Clean Copy, who leads and manages a team of editors who offer an all-in-one editing service, says, "The capacity to understand dense academic text and clarify its meaning without sacrificing nuance" is a definite skill to look for in a copyeditor. She adds, "The editor should have a good ear for the flow of language and strong comprehension skills."

Deepali Joshi, who is a copyediting consultant for the Indian Institute of Management, Bengaluru, and a freelance copyeditor, stresses that copyeditors should "develop the habit of 3Rs: read, re-read, re-re-read." She says, "Never pass a sentence as perfect; always seek to improve the sentence for better readability."

REFERENCE

King S. 2001. *On Writing: a memoir of the craft*, p. xxi. New York: Simon & Schuster. 274 pp.

Venkatesh Krishnamoorthy (kvenkatesh@virtualpaperedit.com) has a master's degree in chemistry and specializes in academic editing in the humanities and social sciences, especially books. After working for over a decade with a few publishing service providers, he became a freelance copyeditor in 2008 and now specializes in editing papers for independent academics. He also takes up independent writing projects.

Vivek Kumar (hivivek72@gmail.com) has a bachelor's degree in science and has more than 25 years of experience as a copyediting professional. He has been working as a freelance medical copyeditor since 2011. He is also the founder of ICF, the Indian Copyeditors Forum: The Forum for Editors.

CHAPTER 4

Credentials in Copyediting

Victoria Bell

OVERVIEW

Editors who hold a credential (such as certification or accreditation) have demonstrated their editorial proficiency through an objective validation of their abilities, usually by a professional editing organization. Earning such a credential can be an important step in an editor's continuing professional development (CPD), both to increase skill in editing and to demonstrate high levels of knowledge to prospective clients and employers.

This chapter describes the following aspects related to credentials in copyediting:

- the benefits of obtaining a credential
- when and how to pursue a credential
- organizations around the world that offer credentialling programmes
- some practical tips when embarking on the journey to obtaining a credential.

Important note: The primary discussion in this chapter deals with certification or accreditation, in the sense of proving one's knowledge and skill through taking an examination or a test, as opposed to earning a certificate by undergoing any training. Some educational resources are included, however.

BENEFITS OF A COPYEDITING CREDENTIAL

Pursuing and obtaining a credential in editing offers several advantages.

Studying for the credential is a form of CPD

Even making the decision to pursue a credential can lead to excellent opportunities for CPD. Studying for a certification or accreditation examination can help editors refresh their editing skills and learn new technology, given that language and editorial techniques are always evolving. Studying can also help editors identify strengths and fill in gaps in their knowledge. Many national or regional associations also have editorial standards, and studying for a credential examination or test is a useful way to become very familiar with them and apply them after the examination.

Some resources for studying and training are covered later in the chapter.

Earning a credential often leads to career advancement for both freelance and in-house editors

Because a respected organization has officially recognized their editing accuracy, judgement, skills, and experience, credentialled editors often find that they have an advantage over editors who do not hold a credential. Credentialled editors may be able to

- charge higher rates
- qualify for better-quality freelance work
- make a strong case for a raise if in full-time employment

- train other editors (leading to a career in teaching, perhaps alongside editing).

Clients and employers who understand the value of a certification or accreditation may prefer a credentialled editor to an uncredentialled one in hiring. Prospective employers may

- seek out editors who advertise their credential in a directory of editors
- not feel the need to set an editing test when considering hiring a credentialled editor
- award higher points to job applicants who are credentialled editors.

Earning a credential benefits the editing profession as a whole

Obtaining a credential requires rigorous studying before the examination. However, the learning process continues after the examination as well. Many credentialling bodies – such as Editors Canada and the Institute of Professional Editors (IPEd) in Australia and New Zealand – require certified or accredited editors to commit to ongoing credential maintenance: every 5 years, these editors must report their editing work and CPD activities. Credential maintenance asks that editors thoughtfully pursue educational opportunities in editing throughout their working lives, which helps to maintain high standards of competence in the editing profession and contributes to raising the profile of professional editors. Earning a credential means that an editor is making an ongoing commitment to the editing profession and their own professional development.

WHEN TO PURSUE AN EDITING CREDENTIAL

There is no denying that registration fees for certification or accreditation examinations are generally steep. (But note that a discount is usually available to an organization's members, which can help.) And the examinations are difficult – as Editors Canada puts it, the certification examination measures excellence, not competence. Moreover, while most examining bodies will allow failing candidates to appeal their grade, an appeal usually involves an additional cost.

For all these reasons, editors should be sure they are ready for the work and expense of tackling an examination.

So, at what stage in their career should editors start thinking about pursuing a credential such as certification or accreditation? It is important to remember that for the most part, the examinations are not designed for entry-level editors.

- Editors Canada recommends that candidates who wish to sit one of its professional certification examinations (in copyediting, proofreading, stylistic editing, or structural editing) have at least 5 years of working experience in the subject area of the examination.
- IPEd notes that candidates should have at least 3 years' experience before sitting its accreditation examination.
- SATI, the South African Translators' Institute, requires 5 years' experience in an editing-related environment, or a higher education qualification in languages or linguistics plus 2 years' experience.
- BELS, the US Board of Editors in the Life Sciences, states that manuscript editors are eligible for certification if they have a bachelor's degree or equivalent from an accredited academic institution and at least 2 years of experience as a manuscript editor in the life sciences.

If you're not ready to pursue a credential yet – or even if you are: some educational resources

Newer editors should consider taking formal training from a reputable organization and gaining more experience before they decide to tackle a certification or accreditation examination. But even seasoned editors can benefit from brushing up on their skills before writing an examination. Many training programmes exist, in a wide range of areas, from months-long programmes to webinars that last just an hour. An in-depth discussion of training in editing is outside the scope of this chapter, but here are some places to start.

- This thorough article features an overview of the pros and cons of taking classes in copyediting (including their fees) and has several links to training and certificate programmes: https://blog.reedsy.com/freelancer/copyediting-certificates/
- An excellent article by Katharine O'Moore-Klopf, a veteran medical editor, covering the differences between education and certification, with many links to training programmes and courses around the world (for both editing and writing): http://www.kokedit.com/ckb_2.php
- Those interested in pursuing training in life-sciences editing might consider the American Medical Writers Association's (despite the name, it is for editors as well!) Essential Skills Certificate: https://www.amwa.org/page/ES_Certificate
- The UK Chartered Institute of Editing and Proofreading (CIEP; formerly SfEP, the Society for Editors and Proofreaders) offers a suite of courses in proofreading, copyediting, and editorial skills at levels ranging from beginner to experienced. Start here: https://www.ciep.uk/training/about-ciep-training-courses/
- Editors Canada has a rolling programme of live webinars, available here: https://training.editors.ca/. A library of previously recorded webinars can be found here: https://training.editors.ca/webinar-recordings/
- The Editorial Freelancers Association provides many resources for editors, from business tips to editing education: https://www.the-efa.org/resources-for-new-freelance-editors/

- IPEd also offers some recorded webinars: https://www.iped-editors.org/professional-development/iped-webinars/
- SATI offers some recorded webinars (including a session related specifically to its accreditation tests) to its members (contact SATI for details at admin@translators.org.za).

CREDENTIALLING PROGRAMMES AROUND THE WORLD

Traditionally, many of the certification or accreditation examinations were administered on paper at a physical examination site. The COVID-19 pandemic has pushed many programmes into adapting to a virtual offering, meaning that more certification programmes are now accessible to international editors than previously. Table 4.1 contains a summary of credentialling programmes in editing around the world: the format, the schedule, who may sit the examination, and fees (as of 2022), where available.

- BELS: Given BELS' definition of a manuscript editor ("concerned not only with the form but with the intellectual content of a manuscript"), it stands to reason that the examination tests a wide range of knowledge relating to manuscripts in the life sciences.
  - The multiple-choice examination focuses on five content domains: mechanics; syntax, clarity, and organization; numbers, measures, statistics, and displays of information; editorial knowledge and judgement; and legal and ethical responsibilities.
  - Full details are available in the section titled 'Defining the Content Domains' in the BELS Study Guide, at this link: https://tinyurl.com/belssg
  - Editors who have at least 2 years of ELS certification and at least 6 years of editorial experience in the life sciences can sit a diplomate examination.
  - See the excellent article by Ravi Murugesan, with further details and a personal account of the experience of taking the BELS examination: https://cutt.ly/owqQ2BpC

Table 4.1 Overview of credentialling programmes worldwide in editing

Examination format	Available to	Fees (as of 2022)
Board of Editors in the Life Sciences, USA https://www.bels.org/earn-your-certification		
Online *or* onsite test centre; 4 times a year; life-sciences editing only	Anyone (requires three letters of reference with application)	US$350
Chartered Institute of Editing and Proofreading, UK https://www.ciep.uk/standards/tests/		
Online basic editorial test; 1 hour *Note:* On the website, CIEP says it is working on an advanced editorial test	Members of CIEP only, as route to upgrading membership and standing in CIEP	£25 per test
Editors Canada, Canada https://www.editors.ca/professional-development/certification		
Professional Certification exams		
Semi–open book (specified study resources allowed); 3-hour examination; onscreen; online. Two examinations annually in November, covering different aspects of editing, on rotating schedule	Anyone, but recommended for editors with 5 or more years of experience	C$450 for members, C$550 for non-members
Editing Essentials test		
Online, multiple-choice, available any time	Anyone, but recommended for editors at the beginning of their careers	C$75 for members, C$100 for non-members

Table 4.1 Overview of credentialling programmes worldwide in editing (*continued*)

Examination format	Available to	Fees (as of 2022)
Institute of Professional Editors, Australia https://www.iped-editors.org/accreditation-scheme/iped-accreditation-exam/		
Open book; 4-hour examination; onscreen; in person (remote option available). One examination every 2 years, covering four categories	IPEd members; members of approved affiliate organizations	A$750
Professional Editors' Guild, South Africa https://editors.org.za/accreditation/		
Open book; onscreen; delivered by email within a specified week, completed test to be returned within 48 hours	Members of PEG (membership for at least 12 months)	ZAR850
South African Translators' Institute, South Africa Members only; contact SATI for details at admin@translators.org.za		
Open book; onscreen; delivered by email on a date agreed upon by the accreditation officer and candidate, returned within 24 hours	Members of SATI (membership for at least 3 months)	ZAR1160 (plus ZAR250 in foreign exchange where applicable)

- CIEP: The editing test covers two main areas: professional practice and editorial knowledge and judgement, which are described in detail in its editorial syllabus available at https://www.ciep.uk/assets/files/public/ciep_editorial_syllabus_v.1.0.pdf "a general range of topics that are considered essential for editorial professionals to know."
- Editors Canada: The organization offers four professional certification examinations (copyediting, structural editing, stylistic editing, and proofreading), as well as the new (online, all multiple-choice) Editing Essentials test, based on the standards delineated in the *Professional Editorial Standards* (2016) (PES-2016): "PES-2016 outlines the range of skills and knowledge editors need. It sets out what editors should do at various stages of editing, and tells employers and clients what to expect from the editors they hire."
  - The professional certification examinations aim to accommodate editors who work in a wide range of fields. Each examination consists of two parts: Part A is a set of multiple-choice and matching questions on the discipline being tested and general knowledge of the publishing process. Part B is always a longer, non-fiction passage to be edited.
- IPEd: The accreditation examination covers the Australian standards for editing practice: https://www.iped-editors.org/about-editing/australian-standards/
  - The examination consists of three parts: language, which tests competence in English (spelling, punctuation, grammar, syntax, and style); knowledge, which tests knowledge of editing and publishing practices; and a manuscript section, which tests practical copyediting skills: making corrections, writing author queries, and creating a style sheet for a short piece of text of a few thousand words.
  - See a candid and very informative article on IPEd accreditation (and much more: working as an editor, preparing for examinations, and the benefits of editing credentials in general) by committee member Linda Nix at https://tinyurl.com/IPEdExam

- PEG: The questions in the accreditation test cover four main areas of the editor's craft: editing (copy, structural, and/or stylistic), proofreading, language (including grammar, spelling, punctuation, word choice), and general (e.g. professional conduct, copyright and plagiarism, US vs UK English, plain language, and specific fields or genres of editing).
- SATI: Most of the information relating to accreditation is available to SATI members only (enquire at admin@translators.org.za), but to our knowledge, the candidate is given six texts to edit in Word, using track changes. SATI does not state specifically what type of editing the examination covers, but from the list of errors that are not allowed, the examination could be described as a test of copyediting or stylistic editing, rather than structural editing.
  - Errors: Producing misleading or unclear text, changing the meaning of the original, deleting vital information, inserting unnecessary information, introducing or not correcting errors of grammar or syntax, introducing or not correcting spelling errors that would not be picked up by a spellchecker, introducing or not correcting inconsistencies, not adhering to accepted conventions, introducing or not correcting errors that render the text inelegant without affecting the message, not correcting spelling errors that would be picked up by a spellchecker.

What can you do with your credential?

- BELS allows board-certified editors to add the letters 'ELS' after their name: Editor in the Life Sciences (or ELS (D), for diplomate-level). Board-certified editors are included in the BELS directory.
- CIEP provides a 'grade-level logo' that members can display on their website and business documents, which "clients in the know will recognize and trust". Professional Members and Advanced Professional Members are included in the CIEP Directory.

- Editors Canada: A candidate who passes each professional certification examination is entitled to the label 'Certified Copyeditor', 'Certified Structural Editor', etc. A candidate who passes all four examinations becomes a 'Certified Professional Editor'. Certified Editors are included in the Roster of Certified Editors.
- IPEd: Accredited Editors may add the letters 'AE' after their names and are included in the Accredited Editors Directory.
- PEG allows accredited editors to add the designation 'Accredited Text Editor' to their email signature and marketing materials from the commencement of the following membership year (i.e. from 1 March).
- SATI: Successful candidates receive an accreditation certificate, their names appear on SATI's list of accredited members, and they may use their SATI accreditation status in communication with clients in an email signature.

PREPARING FOR THE EXAMINATION

Most of the credentialling organizations provide information on how candidates can best prepare for their examination or test. Many of the resources are specific to the organization's country but are useful for editors around the world to prepare for an examination or for general professional development. Some links and pointers are provided below.

- BELS offers a free certification study guide on its website at https://bels.memberclicks.net/study-guide. It covers the fundamentals of how the examination works and provides some sample questions.
- Editors Canada has a subsection of its website dedicated to preparing for the professional certification examination at https://tinyurl.com/EditorsCanada. This page includes

  - a free interactive video on what certification involves, with preparation tips: see 'Video Overview' at https://tinyurl.com/EditorsCanada
  - links to *Test Preparation Guides* (for sale) for each of the four areas examined: these contain sample versions of the examinations but are also good practice for any editing examination
  - lists of useful books and courses, as well as the study guides and dictionaries allowed during the examination
  - tips for studying and preparing for the examination (e.g. study groups), and strategy during the examination
  - tips for studying for the Editing Essentials test: https://tinyurl.com/EditorsCan
  - other relevant publications: https://www.editors.ca/editors-canada-publications
- IPEd offers links to several resources.
  - Study resources for its accreditation examination: https://tinyurl.com/IPEdExamResources. Subjects covered include style guides and handbooks useful for editors worldwide and specific to editors in Australia and New Zealand, a mentorship programme, study groups, and how to work with examination documents (PDF and Word)
  - Links to courses and university programmes (Australia and New Zealand, and worldwide): https://www.iped-editors.org/about-editing/editing-courses/
- PEG appears to offer guides for editors, but these are available to members only.
- SATI does not provide examination preparation resources.

CONCLUSION

There are many good reasons for deciding to pursue a credential in editing, including enhancing job prospects and embarking on a lifelong journey of professional development. But it is important to ask several questions first: Am I ready to undertake a potentially difficult and expensive examination? Where do my strengths and interests lie: do I want to specialize in a particular subject area (such as medical copyediting), and if so, should I pursue a credential through one specific organization over another, or sit one type of examination rather than another (e.g. to go for a copyediting credential vs a general editing one)? How best can I prepare: what resources do I need for studying? It is our hope that some of the advice in this chapter will be of practical help to editors who are trying to answer these questions as they step onto the path of earning a credential. Best of luck!

Victoria Bell (info@vmbell.com) is a Certified Professional Editor (a certification awarded by Editors Canada) and was the co-chair (2019–2021) of the Editors Canada Certification Steering Committee. Currently based in Ottawa, Canada, she works for the *Canadian Medical Association Journal* and is also a freelance copyeditor of fiction.

PART II

Editorial Niches

CHAPTER 5

Academic Editing

Suraj Mylapore

Academic editing occupies a niche in the broader field of editing. This chapter discusses the salient principles of academic editing.

ACADEMIC RIGOUR

While the word *academic* has different meanings in different contexts, Merriam-Webster defines it to be 'based on formal study especially at an institution of higher learning' (https://www.merriam-webster.com/dictionary/ under the headword academic used as an adjective, as in academic editing). Academic editing refers to editing scientific literature, such as articles in academic journals and discipline-specific scholarly and encyclopaedic works.

Academic copyediting involves copyediting manuscripts authored and submitted by research professionals, scientists, and scholars to professional publication houses, typically journal offices, university presses, professional associations, and commercial for-profit publishing enterprises. Academic copyediting requires that the copyeditor maintain high standards of consistency and clarity, because academic publications are indispensable to the worldwide dissemination of the knowledge established by researchers and academics.

EXPERTISE IN SUBJECT MATTER

Copyediting, academic or otherwise, may be broadly categorized into two types, namely technical and non-technical: in the former, the copyeditor needs to be a subject matter expert on the content being copyedited, while this is not a mandatory requirement in the latter.

Sometimes, a publisher requests a mechanical check of the content. This task is not the same as a technical edit and usually goes by the term *fact check* or *accuracy check*. In a text on history, for example, a fact check may entail locating authentic online sources that support all the facts stated in the text. Accuracy checks are often made on textbooks on software applications.

- For a text on software programming, for example, an accuracy check would mean a step-by-step verification that all of the algorithms in the text indeed yield the results as indicated in the text.
- For a text on Microsoft Excel, for example, accuracy checkers would install the application on their device and verify that each of the features and functionalities listed in the text are in fact found on the software application.

Accuracy checks are also often made on texts on the STEM disciplines (short for 'science, technology, engineering, math' disciplines), which carry numerical exercises and problems along with their solutions.

GRAMMAR AND MARKUP

No matter how accurate and robust the experimental method, how precise the observation and collation of data, and how sound the analysis of results in a scientific work, if the description of the experiment, observation, and inference – the writing – is not as exact and robust, the published work may not be well received or appreciated or, indeed, may not even be well understood. Copyeditors therefore play a role of immeasurable value in the publication of academic and scientific work.

A grammar check and markup are two tasks a copyeditor executes. Markup comes first and refers to the so-called mechanical aspects of copyediting. It involves (1) identifying each and every element in the text, such as heading levels, paragraphs, figure captions, and source lines and (2) imposing consistency upon the manuscript. A grammar check comprises a line-by-line reading of the entire text to ensure that all errors of grammar, spelling, sense, and internal contradictions are removed.

Ensuring good grammar and correct spellings are two essentials of copyediting. Although pruning redundant text is a favourite among some copyeditors (changing 'in order to' to 'to', for instance), more importantly, they spot what is missing, which could often be a straightforward verb error but may well turn out to be something subtle, something that a word processor would not spot; consider, for example, the following sentence: 'Capital punishment is our society's recognition of the paucity of human life.' Although the sentence is grammatically correct, it lacks sense – unless the copyeditor replaces 'paucity' with 'sanctity'.

At advanced levels of copyediting, a flawed argument or discussion would need to be corrected or flagged for the author's attention: for example, a passage that discusses the causes of the Second World War but leaves out the effect the Great Depression had on ordinary Germans. Obvious errors of fact would also need to be corrected. If an author inadvertently places the decimal incorrectly while stating the mass of the proton, the copyeditor needs to catch the error: 1.673×10^{-27} kg or 16.73×10^{-27} kg? Gross historical errors would also need to be removed or flagged. What follows is a serious historical typo, so to speak: 'Napoleon fought his last battle, at Waterloo, on

15 June 1715': an alert copyeditor would catch the typo and change '1715' to '1815'.

In the context of correcting gross factual errors, copyeditors of today are largely helped by web searches, an advantage their predecessors from, say, two decades ago did not enjoy.

CONSISTENCY AND HOUSE STYLE

Common to both markup and the grammar check is the requirement of consistency – an important aspect of editing – and style. Writing 'five children' in one chapter and '8 children' in another appears somehow troubling to the human mind: we find a text trustworthy only if we see uniformity and predictability in it, which may explain the overwhelming significance attached to consistency in a copyedit. Of course, consistent presentation makes life easier for the reader; for example, finding '500 kWh/day', '500 kilowatt-hours per day', and '500 kWh d^{-1}' at different instances of the same text not only confuses the reader but also accurately reflects the lack of coherence and standardization in the mind of the author and that of the copyeditor. The treatment of all textual items that appear in the work needs to be made consistent, according to the publisher's house style or any other approved style: the treatment of numbers, ages, complex numerical data, tables and illustrations, initialisms and abbreviations, currency, percentages and fractions, dates, and so forth.

Style refers to a preference with respect to how an element of text is presented on a printed page or a web page, setting level 1 headings in headline style, for example. House style refers to the consolidated preference of a particular publishing house on how their content needs to be typeset. Now, the textual attributes that control the presentation of text are many, such as typeface (e.g. Times New Roman, Calibri), point size, vertical or horizontal spacing before and after the element, capitalization (e.g. all caps, headline style, or sentence style), font style (roman or italics), and even font colour. Deciding which combination of textual attributes would apply to a particular textual element – in our example, all level 1 heads in the manuscript – is akin to deciding on the style for that element. In a nutshell, style is the combination of textual attributes by which every element in text is presented with or identified by on the printed page.

Note that while a copyeditor decides that a head is a level 1 head, it is the typesetter who makes sure that the approved design for the level 1 head – the textual attributes mentioned earlier that control the presentation of text – is in fact applied on the typeset pages during typesetting. For example, in this chapter, all level 1 heads have been set in all-caps style. For online-only publications, copyeditors use a document called a cascading style sheet to execute this task.

ACADEMIC TEXTS

Academic publications are broadly divided into two types: books and periodicals. Sometimes, voluminous reports, for example those published by an extra-governmental body such as the United Nations, may also be of an academic nature.

Books might run anywhere from a hundred pages to thousands of pages, whereas articles in academic journals seldom go beyond fifty pages and are typically no more than ten pages. Journals are published primarily for disseminating currently evolving knowledge. Because journals are the primary medium through which research findings are shared across the research world, they need to be published pretty quickly. *Speed to print* is the operative term here. As Sir Isaac Newton acknowledged, 'If I have seen further, it is by standing on the shoulders of giants.' This statement expressly reflects how the building of knowledge develops by collaboration between several research bodies, hence the critical nature of academic publications in the dissemination of knowledge, as noted earlier in this chapter.

Journal articles are meant for a very specific readership of subject matter experts and discipline specialists in a particular field of work, typically research workers and scholars, as discussed before; journals such as the *American Journal of Anthropology* and *Nature* fall in this category.

General-interest magazines of an academic nature are meant for the more general reader interested in academic content or with a scientific temper. Such magazines do not assume discipline-specific expertise in their readers. *Scientific American* and *Science News* are widely respected publications that fall in this category.

Books, on the other hand, focus on elucidation and in-depth treatment of a subject, usually pertaining to content that falls within the purview of established knowledge – knowledge beyond dispute at the time of writing. This is particularly true of pedagogical works, intended for consumption by students in universities and similar such institutions of higher learning. While copyediting pedagogical works, copyeditors need to impose clarity and precision on the text. In short, if you wish to be updated on the most recent developments in a particular field of work, you would consult a relevant journal. Journals represent the frontiers of contemporary knowledge. On the other hand, if you need an exhaustive treatment of a subject, you would reach out for a good book on the subject.

CLARITY AND BREVITY: THE SOUL OF ACADEMIC EXPRESSION

Simplicity is the hallmark of good academic writing. It follows that copyeditors need to ensure that their copyedited content is clear and crisp, requiring minimal effort on the part of the reader to understand the content. For a taste of how bad academic writing can sometimes be, try reading these passages.

- I shall not seek to determine the questions of how far fears of aggression by Carthage, by Hellenistic kingdoms, or later by northern or eastern peoples provided Rome with motives for an expansionist posture, as it appears apparent that they all too often provided pretexts and excuses for belligerence, or of how far the real cause of expansion must be sought in the merest of desires for blood, power, and glory.

- Statutes, policies, concords, and procedures drafted with the objective of helping to prevent large-volume shootings and reducing or moderating their lethality when they do occur that are based upon highly inaccurate stereotypes, uninformed political agenda, inflated fear, and raw emotion can never or seldom be successful or if they are unlikely to last for a significant period of time.

As an example of editing for clarity, the first of these examples may be revised as shown here, and you are encouraged to try your hand with the second example.

- It appears that much of Rome's belligerence and expansionist posture was due to its own desire for blood, power, and glory and less to fears of aggression from foreign kingdoms, namely Carthage and the Hellenistic kingdoms or later the northern or eastern peoples.

It is important to note here that a copyeditor may make such revisions only with express permission from the publisher; such requirements and expectations are usually included in the project-related instructions the copyeditor receives before beginning work. At the minimum, however, the copyeditor must correct outright errors of grammar, spelling, and consistency.

An excellent text that helps copyeditors master their trade is Strunk and White's classic work *The Elements of Style*. Following are a few of the important rules elucidated in that text (Strunk and White 1920/1999).

- Use the active voice.
- Put statements in positive form.
- Use definite, specific, concrete language; compare 'A period of unfavourable weather set in' and 'It rained every day for a week.'
- Omit needless words.
- Keep related words together.
- Write with nouns and verbs.

SOURCES, PEER REVIEW, AND PERMISSIONS

Sources

Citing sources and providing references plays a crucial role in disseminating academic knowledge. A reference is a collection of items of bibliographic information that are sufficient for the reader to locate the work being cited.

In academic work, providing evidence for every statement made is mandatory. Authors are even expected to supply the manufacturer's name with regard to the equipment and disposables used in their experimental work.

Sources may be cited either as reference citations or as notes (footnotes or endnotes). This book uses references.

Here is a list of the components, or bibliographic details, that make up a reference to a source.

- Name(s) of the author(s)
- Title of the work and year of publication
- Information on the publisher or the cited work that helps the reader locate the source; such information is different for different types of sources.
  - **Print book:** simply the publisher's name and location.
  - **Journal article:** the title of the journal, volume number, and page numbers. For a greater understanding of how journal articles are compiled and released as issues, you may simply visit the websites

of some popular journal databases (e.g. Genamics JournalSeek; http://journalseek.net).
- **Newspaper:** The exact date of publication, the city – because most national newspapers have different editions for different cities – and page number, and sometimes column number.
- **Proceedings of a conference or a symposium:** The title of the symposium followed by its location and the date.
- **Online sources:** The URL of the web page.

The following examples illustrate reference patterns depending on the type of work. The work used in these examples is a fictitious work by Sir Isaac Newton.

- **Book:** Newton, Isaac (2023), *Why the apple fell down*, Londonium, Apple Publishers.
- **Journal:** Newton, Isaac (2023), 'Why the apple fell down,' *Principia*, 1, 10–12.
- **Newspaper:** Newton, Isaac (2023), 'Why the apple fell down,' *Principia News*, 4 June, pp. 10–12.
- **Proceedings of a conference:** Newton, Isaac (2023), 'Why the apple fell down,' Proceedings of the Society for Natural Philosophy, Londonium, 4–10 June.
- **Online:** Newton, Isaac (2023), 'Why the apple fell down,' https://apples-and-oranges.com/why-the-apple-fell-down.

The sources may be cited in text as direct citations or as indirect citations, for example, as noted here:

- **Direct citation:** Newton (2023) propounded the laws of motion for macroscopic bodies.
- **Indirect citation:** The laws of motion for macroscopic bodies were propounded (Newton, 2023).

These examples follow the Harvard system of references, also known as the name–year system of references or the author–date system of references.

Peer review

Another process essential to academic publishing goes by the term *peer review*. Every academic work goes through one or more rounds of peer review, which removes the possibility of bias in the process of evaluation of the manuscript. A peer review can be of two types.

- In a single-blind peer review, the identity of the reviewers is withheld from the authors while the reviewers are aware of who the authors are.
- In a double-blind peer review, the identity of both parties is unknown to each other: neither the reviewers nor the authors are aware of each other's identity.

The benefit of a peer review is that the manuscript is validated by experienced and knowledgeable experts in the same field of work for factual correctness and experimental rigour. Only if the manuscript passes such a review is it considered ready for copyediting and publication. Therefore, when authors cite such peer-reviewed works to support their argument, the latter is considered valid by the wider academic community. The cited sources, as described earlier, may be books and monographs, journal articles, magazines and newspapers, or reports. However, in academic work, journal articles and, to a lesser extent, books form the staple of most of the sources cited. A case in point is the widely used online encyclopaedia Wikipedia: although popular with the general public, it is rarely cited in academic publications because its entries are not peer reviewed.

Permissions

Permissions here simply refers to fair and legally tenable reuse of content from an external source in an author's text. Before an author publishes content from another source – either text or art – the author must obtain permission, if necessary upon payment of a fee, from the entity that owns the copyright to the content the author desires to reproduce. However, if the authors can prove that they are reusing copyrighted content purely for non-profit purposes, the use may be considered 'fair use' and does not require payment. Acknowledgement of source is mandatory in all circumstances, regardless of whether reuse required payment of a fee or not. This arrangement is subject to the agreement between the author and the copyright owner. This part of the publication process is generally completed before copyediting begins.

The copyeditor holds the responsibility to flag permissions and copyright issues arising because of non-compliance with the permissions paperwork supplied by the publisher. At the time of transmitting a work to the copyeditor, most often the publisher has already ascertained that the author has obtained the permissions to reproduce any copyrighted content. The copyeditor is supplied with the relevant information, such as textual items or images that require permission and details of the acknowledgement of their source. The paperwork related to permissions usually includes, among others, a label for the image or textual piece, the name of the copyright owner, and the exact wording of acknowledgement specified by the copyright owner to be published along with the reproduced content. It is the copyeditor's responsibility to ensure that these items – as detailed in the publisher's permissions document – are correctly incorporated in the manuscript.

The Chicago Manual of Style (The University of Chicago Press 2017), now in its 17th edition, presents as excellent overview of this topic, which you are encouraged to consult.

CONCLUSION

Academic copyediting forms an important part of the process of disseminating scholarly knowledge and is based on the same rules of scholarship and rigour that are the foundation of academic research. Academic copyediting is not only a personally fulfilling profession but also one that serves the progress of knowledge in the world.

REFERENCES

The University of Chicago Press. 2017. *The Chicago Manual of Style*, 17th edn. Chicago: The University of Chicago Press. 1144 pp.

Strunk W and White E B. 1920/1999. *The Elements of Style*, 4th edn. Boston, MA: Allyn & Bacon. 105 pp.

Suraj Mylapore (surajmylapore@gmail.com) is an editorial professional with more than 20 years of experience. He specializes in advanced copyediting and content services, both in humanities and in medical and STEM publishing, covering different types of publications. Suraj has set up copyediting teams, designing and overseeing successful implementation of all processes right from the drawing board, which outlines the management's vision, to sustained deliveries on the ground. Among the editorial deliverables he values most is the copyediting training programme he has developed over the course of his career. Suraj holds a master's degree in physics from the University of Madras and lives in Chennai, India.

CHAPTER 6

Editing Schoolbooks: An Insider's Story

Soma Bhattacharjya

Our present-day world is dynamic. It changes and expands quickly because of various influences and improvements in our day-to-day lives. Expanding horizons of knowledge and information affect our lives and lead to continual evaluation of our skills and their applications.

The world of making books, too, has evolved over time. The traditional image of books as carriers of facts, data, and study matter has undergone a sea change – today, we can safely say that everything is potential material for learning. So, whether we are looking at the content of books or advertising jingles or electronic media, we are actually interacting with materials in different formats suited to different learning purposes and real-life needs!

WORLD OF TEXTBOOKS

There are different kinds of books as there are different kinds of readers. Readers select books based on the purpose of their reading. Thus we have educational books and books for hobbies or for pleasure.

Books for educational purposes are designed especially to meet the requirements of a given syllabus and curriculum. Such books, which are generally used by students, are easy to handle, simply written, and largely examination oriented. For the purposes of this chapter, I focus only on school textbooks as representative of educational books without touching upon college-level textbooks in detail.

SCHOOL TEXTBOOKS

School textbooks cater to the processes of teaching and learning involving children up to their teenage years. These books are written so as to comply with set guidelines for scholastic pursuits. The guidelines are designed in terms of learning objectives in the cognitive, intellectual, and psychomotor domains.

Who writes schoolbooks?

Like any other book which is 'written', schoolbooks, too, are written. Traditionally, publishers would connect with and commission schoolteachers to develop content since it was believed that they have the understanding and knowledge of content for schoolbooks to work. This logic stood the test of time as schoolteachers had the experience of classroom management in terms of handling various types of students and making classrooms meaningful by choosing appropriate content.

However, as the business of publishing schoolbooks became more and more challenging, with markets becoming more and more dynamic, developing schoolbooks also became more complicated, although more interesting, with evolved workflow processes and ecosystems. Content, layout, support systems – all underwent changes to suit new demands and expectations.

Over the years a new class of specialists has also emerged, namely content specialists, who may work independently or may be employed by agencies that, although not schools, understand what content works at what level and are also familiar with syllabi and student assessment. Sometimes, publishers collaborate with such specialists to 'author' books and typically change their business models to suit whomsoever they are working with.

Schoolbooks versus books for higher studies

At this point, it is important to distinguish between schoolbooks or textbooks and educational books for colleges and higher studies. In India, schoolbooks are designed according to the guidelines set by NCERT, the National Council of Educational Research and Training. The curricula are centralized and binding on all involved in school education. With books for higher studies, on the other hand, the content is determined not just by the defined curricular goals but also according to needs as visualized by any given university. The expectations to meet uniform learning outcomes across regions and locations may not be homogeneous in books for higher education, and some academic books focus on specialized research in specific disciplines.

School textbooks further differ from higher academic books in terms of page layout, artwork, and illustrations. Schoolbooks are elaborately illustrated, make generous use of colour, and strive for attractive appearance; books for higher studies, on the other hand, contain scientific drawings and information presented as tables, and feature staid rather than vibrant layouts. School textbooks are typically demy quarto, that is about 8¾ × 11¼ inches, whereas supplementary readers, which are smaller, typically demy octavo, that is about 5¾ × 8½ inches (Ritter 2002). One may not find such uniformity in books for colleges and beyond.

Defining the editor in the publishing process

The publisher–author relationship is important in the conception of a book: the publisher judges market needs and possible returns, whereas the author lends a vision to the business plan. Content, supporting evidence, illustrations, references, contrasts, comparisons – all stem from the author's vision and plan: the publisher joins the dots and makes that plan a reality.

It is in this finely balanced equation that the editor assumes importance. The editor works closely with the author on behalf of the publisher. He or she understands the vision and works for mutual benefits. The editor presents the author's ethereal ideas to the publisher for turning them into material objects, namely books, which can then be made available to the target readership.

Role of the schoolbooks editor

An editor for schoolbooks performs all the above functions, but with a difference, for a few good reasons. First, schoolbook publishing is curriculum driven. Second, school publishing is locale-specific: I distinguish it here from custom publishing, which is very client-specific and tailored to the needs of a specified market. Third, in terms of business, in custom publishing the collaborating agency has a greater say in determining costs and prices.

Against this background, the role of the schoolbooks editor becomes complex and exciting as well. He or she becomes the in-house agent for determining content, layout, artwork – indeed the carrier and promoter of a vision that potentially affects a large number of people. A schoolbooks editor is responsible for making quality checks on various aspects of the books so that the right impressions are formed in the minds of the formative learners, who are the main users of such books. Needless to say, the schoolbooks editor must have knowledge and understanding of age- and level-specific current school curricula and their requirements.

Here are the more important functions of a schoolbooks editor.

- Study the prescribed syllabus.
- Know the competing titles.
- Study the competition.

- Formulate unique selling propositions for a given course.
- Review manuscripts.
- Give feedback to authors.
- Identify scope of artwork.
- Develop artwork briefs.
- Evaluate a manuscript to ensure that all learning outcomes desirable for each stage are achieved.
- Edit a manuscript to fulfil the requirements of the curriculum.
- Ensure stylistic consistency.
- Develop a path for smooth movement of proofs through various stages.
- Submit error-free last proof to the publisher to consider for printing.

Based on the above job description of an editor, the essential qualifications of an editor may be listed as follows:

- Postgraduate qualification in the required subject (essential)
- Degree in education (desirable)
- Exposure to essentials of book production including editing, preferably through a course or programme of study (desirable).

DEVELOPING SCHOOLBOOKS

The development of schoolbooks follows a similar workflow as that for other books. The flowchart given in Figure 6.1 gives a rough idea of the workflow.

As is clear from the figure, producing schoolbooks is an elaborate process, too complex to be handled by a single editor alone. A hierarchy of editors generally work simultaneously to develop textbooks (it must be remembered that schoolbooks are developed in a series, allowing editors to work simultaneously on many titles). Thus, while one editor may edit the manuscript, another may develop the brief for

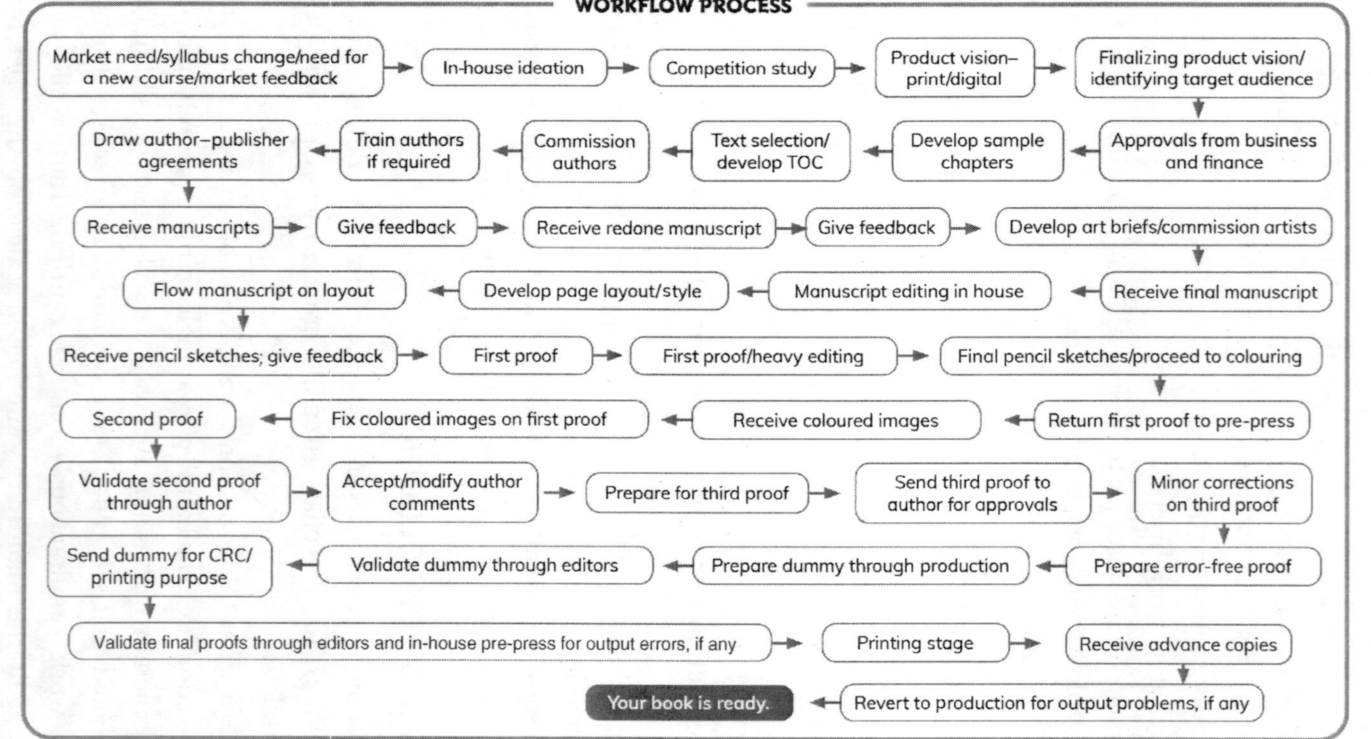

Figure 6.1 The development of a book: from conception to publication. *CRC*, Camera-ready copy; *TOC*, table of contents.

the artist and yet another may apply for permissions to reproduce copyrighted material, for example, permissions from the Survey of India for reproducing maps of India. Another set of editors may be busy adding content, checking facts, or developing answer keys to the end-of-the-lesson questions. Schoolbooks production, especially the editorial department, is a dynamic place where ideation, discussion, and the way forward are chartered to add to the corpus of knowledge.

EDITING SCHOOLBOOKS: SOME POINTERS

The parameters of editing are set at the time of developing sample lessons. Authors are made conscious of things to watch out for while writing content, such as adhering to a specific syllabus, ensuring desired learning outcomes, keeping within the word limit for each chapter or lesson, choosing appropriate examples, and keeping in mind the sociocultural background of learners. Thus, by the time editing in real terms begins, that is, once the author submits a complete manuscript, the editor examines it against a set checklist and first of all spots any gaps in received matter. Secondly, the editor maps learning outcomes as shown by the author to learning indicators as defined by the syllabus guidelines, which are binding upon all.

With these phases completed, the editor sets himself or herself the task of 'editing' the content, which includes checking for language use appropriate to the specified level, accuracy of facts and definitions, suitability of examples, coherence and logic, the level of difficulty of tasks and exercises, and clarity in explaining concepts. The editor meticulously marks – and if possible fills – any gaps in communication while being careful not to overload the teaching points in each lesson. In editing schoolbooks, the editor constantly switches between being an editor and being a content creator: in spotting errors, the editor performs the role of an editor; however, when the same editor inserts additional text or rewrites chunks of content to suit the overall design of the book, he or she becomes a content creator. The specialized role of the editor goes further in determining the style and artwork for books, wherein the editor ensures consistency and adherence to selected artwork and colouring styles decided upon while finalizing the art brief.

Challenges in schoolbook editing

Challenges in schoolbook editing begin from inception. As defined earlier, schoolbooks are framed with federal guidelines but with localized flavours (localized in the sense that they cater largely to a defined political boundary and are rarely prepared with a foreign market in mind). For example, schoolbooks developed by leading publishing houses in India will cater to students within India most of the time. Spin-off courses from main programmes of study may be designed for specific audiences in India or neighbouring countries, but only sometimes. Therefore, the test that an editor must pass consists in achieving a balance between various sociocultural aspects of society while achieving the desired learning outcomes stated in policy documents.

Secondly, not all programmes of study are meant for the same audience. Just as a society itself is heterogeneous, so are the products meant for schools, in that they must satisfy the learning needs of different profiles of learners with varied learning objectives. An editor placed in such a situation must have a clear understanding of the learner profile in terms of what the learners are already expected to know and what the expected learning outcomes are. Accordingly, an editor of schoolbooks strives to deliver a product appropriate in terms of content, language use, and assessment exercises while making judicious decisions related to course delivery that is advantageous to both the publisher and the buyer. To illustrate this point, should a publisher decide to make a language-learning course for upper-middle-class learners seeking to expand their employment opportunities, the publisher must choose between making the courseware entirely print based or a mix of print and digital forms. Further, the publisher may have to decide which skills to develop through the print medium and which may be developed more effectively by using digital content. Through all such deliberations, the editor needs to deliver conscientious and informed inputs to ensure that the selected learning model does not fail.

Thirdly, taking off from the previous point, language editing forms an important aspect in schoolbooks and is not limited merely to appropriate vocabulary and correct syntax and structure but also considers the learners' stock of active and passive vocabulary and encourages them to transfer the ever-increasing proportion of their passive vocabulary to their active vocabulary. Language editing also includes removing ambiguities and resolving obstacles to communication by making instructions simple, straightforward, and clear.

TRENDS

We live in rapidly changing times. We have survived a worldwide pandemic, namely COVID-19, and its deadly complications, which have not only destabilized our lives but also forced us to redesign and redefine our lives and systems within which we operate.

Our work lives, too, have changed. Working from home, for example, is the new reality. Against this background, we need to appreciate the pointers to changes in the development of schoolbooks. With the entire population homebound for two years, learning was confined to the home. Learners adapted to learning from home through virtual classrooms equipped with digital assets. This led to a spurt in remote learning models and self-learning models, indeed a whole gamut of assets under the umbrella of machine-assisted learning. Schoolbook publishing has certainly found new vistas in content curation and delivery mechanisms. Whether it is content for learners or teachers, experts in schoolbook publishing have evolved to meet the demands of the times. The number of players, too, has increased over time. Today there are more publishers, content development agencies, and assessment specialists than ever before, offering solutions to learners. The times ahead are challenging and educative as well.

To elaborate on trends and the way forward in schoolbook publishing, I reproduce below some excerpts from an interview with Harish Singh Bora, Business Head, Sky Books, recorded on 23 December 2021.

Question 1. Traditional models of sales support have had to be modified during the pandemic. How have you supplemented for the loss of human touch or intervention in recent times?

Well, to my understanding there hasn't been a loss of human touch in literal terms although physical interaction in classrooms had been affected temporarily. However, educators across the country did adapt to the virtual classroom models or hybrid classroom models that are still prevalent. This has prompted the facilitators (like us publishers) to be more pragmatic in the delivery of tools (digital or otherwise) that supplement the new teaching media. So, on the one hand, while creating user-friendly interfaces for all digital assets is now a responsibility, on the other hand, creating content for intended learning to achieve optimal outcomes is a greater responsibility because the user is (now more than ever before) evaluating the benefits in clear, tangible terms.

In simpler terms, the sales support now has to be more functional in approach and flexible enough to incorporate solutions without stretching the budget that affects the overall profitability in operations.

Question 2. Are users prepared for new models of sales support? What evolution in roles do you expect from publishers?

Yes; in our experience the users are indeed prepared for new models of sales support in terms of all products and services offered to them. The role of a publisher is now evolving towards becoming a true academic partner to institutions (schools) and providing 360-degree solutions instead of being merely a product seller.

Question 3. What impact will the new methods in sales-support activities have on editorial departments, which have been considered as largely back-office operations?

Well, to my mind, editorial isn't just a back-office operation; anyone who thinks so doesn't fully understand the term 'quality' (with respect to content creation). There has always been a great deal of thought, research, and creativity that go into making good content and it is the editorial that takes on this mantle.

The new methods in sales-support activities only further strengthen the need for a quality editorial team so that there is no room for mediocrity. Any good educational course that is accepted by educators and learners throughout the world is by itself a testimony to great editorial work put together by the team of editors and authors (here I would include authors as being part of the editorial team).

Question 4. Do you expect a rise in interest in school publishing? Why or why not?

In my opinion this is the perfect time for companies who have love for education especially in the K-12 segment to invest their time, money, and resources in school publishing in India. This is a time that will establish quality over the mediocrity that crept into the educational publishing domain because of undesirable practices such as booksellers using content available on the internet to publish books and claim to be publishers. There are many examples of small-time traders who ventured into educational publishing taking this route and were able to infiltrate and influence the buying behaviour of institutions through unethical means. Thankfully, we have now entered a phase in which, henceforth, good content will reign supreme. Content will be king.

CONCLUSION

Schoolbooks offer an exciting and fruitful enterprise for all stakeholders: the joy of developing content that works and makes an impact on the learner is difficult to capture in words. Gone are the days when learners relied on a single book as the primary source of information. Learners need to juggle between multiple sources of information. Schoolbooks, therefore, should be dynamic to cater to the life needs of learners. Schoolbooks, in today's context, need to reflect the aspirations of young learners while upholding eternal values of good citizenship and healthy co-existence.

REFERENCE

Ritter R M. 2002. *The Oxford Guide to Style*, p. 24. Oxford: Oxford University Press. 624 pp.

Soma Bhattacharjya (soma.bhattacharjya@hotmail.com) is a writer and editor of English-language teaching materials. She holds a PhD in English and a Certificate in Teaching English as a Second Language. She has trained in various English-language teaching (ELT) methods in India and was a recipient of a British Council fellowship for a course on material writing for second-language learners in Leeds, UK. She has worked in different editorial capacities in leading publishing houses. At present, she works in the editorial department of Sky Books, Delhi.

CHAPTER 7

Introduction to Copyediting Fiction

Dola Basu Singh

Only God gets it right the first time and only a slob says,
"Oh well, let it go, that's what copyeditors are for."

– Stephen King[1]

Although Stephen King's advice is for writers, it also highlights the importance of copyeditors, who are, indeed, the force that prevents writers from appearing sloppy to readers. Copyediting fiction and copyediting non-fiction have a lot in common – both need an eye for detail, deep knowledge of the language, and commitment to the reader. Despite these similarities there are enough differences that can overwhelm, and often deter, professionals from taking up fiction editing. The aim of this chapter is to explain the many aspects of copyediting fiction that set it apart from copyediting non-fiction, so that novice fiction editors or experienced non-fiction editors who want to make a career switch find the world of copyediting fiction easier to navigate.

1 King (2000).

LEVELS OF FICTION EDITING

Editing is not a catch-all activity that can take a book from its first draft to being publish-worthy in a single pass. The required work goes on at two levels – the story-wide level and the sentence level – and both need a specialist focus. Editing at the story-wide level is editing the big picture – it ensures that the book works as a whole; editing at the sentence level is editing at the micro level – by focusing on correct use of language, clarity, and readability, it ensures that the readers do not trip up while reading.

The big-picture level: developmental editing, manuscript critique, sensitivity reading

Developmental editing

Developmental editing is a type of big-picture editing that is variously known as content editing, structural editing, substantive editing, or book doctoring. Whatever term you use, it is important to list what the service entails in detail for the benefit of your clients. This is especially relevant in case you want to work for independent or self-published authors who might not have the traditional publishing background and support. They may not know what term to use to indicate the level of intervention they are looking for or they might be confused and use an incorrect term when they mean something else altogether. In a developmental edit the editor looks at story-wide issues for the novel as a whole. This can include identifying holes in the plot, issues with story structure, weak characters, etc. The editor makes comments on the manuscript itself whenever an issue arises, usually working scene by scene, and may change some of the text as an example to demonstrate the point, but thorough sentence-level work is not the focus of a developmental edit. In addition to comments, the editor writes a detailed editorial report of their findings and impressions.

Manuscript critique

Another form of big-picture editing is called manuscript evaluation, manuscript critique, or editorial review. In providing this service, the editor reads the manuscript and reports their findings in a detailed editorial report. This is a great option for authors to get feedback on their early drafts, especially when they want to test their idea but it is too early to invest in a full developmental edit. Authors who need a developmental edit but have a lower budget often choose this option.

Sensitivity reading

Yet another kind of edit within the category of big-picture editing is sensitivity reading, which involves the editor reading the book while keeping an eye out for offensive content, misrepresentation, stereotypes, bias, etc. They write a report outlining the problems they find and offer solutions.

The Sentence level: line editing, copyediting, proofreading

Line editing

Line editing is the stage at which the editor makes sure that the flow of the story as well as the language is smooth and that everything makes sense. Line editing shares some common ground with both developmental editing and copyediting. The aim of line editing is dual: to fix story-level as well as sentence-level issues. Line editing fixes such problems as awkward phrasing, clichés, misused words, and inappropriate tone along with plot-based inconsistencies, unintentional ambiguities, and minor holes in the plot. Line editing makes sure the sentences convey the author's intended meaning, and that there is no repetition or redundancy to make the reading experience tedious. The ultimate purpose is to have a story the readers can immerse themselves in.

Copyediting

Copyediting is the correcting stage during which the editor corrects errors or inconsistencies in grammar, punctuation, style, etc. Copyediting is also the stage at which fact-checking and plagiarism checks are carried out. However, the role of the fiction copyeditor is not limited to these tasks: the fiction copyeditor also needs to ensure consistency in character names and traits, the timeline of the story and the plot, etc. It is important to remember that many fiction editors often combine their line and copyediting services into a single service and call it either line editing or copyediting because both go hand in hand. It is therefore most important to let the author know in detail all the tasks that a service is expected to cover.

Proofreading

Proofreading is the final stage of the editorial process, the stage that ensures quality control and during which any remaining errors or layout problems are flagged so that the book becomes fit for publication.

QUALITIES OF A GOOD FICTION COPYEDITOR

As discussed above, a good fiction copyeditor fixes much more than grammar, spelling, punctuation, and style. Therefore, let us discuss the general approach and mindset that good fiction copyeditors must possess in order to serve their authors' best interests.

- Good fiction copyeditors are first of all readers. The idea of spending our professional lives reading romances or mysteries or some other favourite genre and getting paid for it is thrilling, and although editors are aware that there is more to copyediting than simply reading the story, there is no denying the fact that the love of reading a wide variety of genres and authors plays an important role in fiction editing. I will even go out on a limb to say that every good fiction editor is also a reader. Every genre has some conventions and tropes that readers immediately recognize and even look for when seeking out a new book. Reading widely in a given genre gives us a sense of what works in a story and what does not, and how different authors use the same universal tropes in their own unique ways.

- Successful fiction copyeditors have the inherent sense to recognize a good story. Knowing the art and craft of writing helps tremendously. A great way to familiarize yourself would be to enrol in a creative writing course or read books aimed at improving the writer's craft. Authors read such books and apply the principles they learn to their own writing, and many would expect their editor to understand where they are coming from.
- Good fiction copyeditors do their best to preserve the authors' unique voice (or even help them develop it) while making sure the story elements are working. 'This is not my book' is a great mantra to live by for fiction copyeditors, especially if they are also writers themselves. Remember that your job is to help authors tell their story the best way they can, not change things just because it does not suit your ideas.
- Good fiction editors query their authors in a kind and sensitive manner. A work of fiction is much more personal than an academic book, and most fiction is drawn from real life (often from the author's own). The theme, the story, the characters may be inspired by real life. The book in your hand may be part of a bigger dream. Being sensitive towards these aspects makes for better queries. It takes great courage to put your creation out in the world for everyone to see, and the least we can do is to be on the writer's side and offer kind, constructive feedback.
- Good copyeditors do not fix what is not broken. The rules of grammar, punctuation, or style are much more fluid for fiction than for non-fiction. You may encounter 'incorrect' grammar or usage in dialogue or in a first-person narrative, but are those

really mistakes? An uneducated Texan geezer can hardly be expected to speak the same way an English professor would. The addition or removal of a single comma for the sake of being 'correct' may alter the tension or the tone dramatically. So, it becomes really important to move beyond prescriptivism and strike a balance between what the dictionary or a style guide prescribes and what the character and the story demand, especially if you are a stickler for language.

- Good fiction copyeditors do not apply their own moral code to the book at hand. Unlike most non-fiction, you will most certainly come across curse words, blasphemy, sex scenes, and unpleasant acts in fiction. You may choose not to accept manuscripts that contain such acts, but once you do accept a manuscript, your job is to copyedit without letting your own moral code get in the way.

COPYEDITING FICTION

Now let us assume you have landed a fiction copyediting project. So, what are the next steps? What is it you should be looking to do (or not do), and how do you go about doing those things?

As a fiction copyeditor, you would do all the things a non-fiction copyeditor does. You will check for correct spelling, grammar, punctuation, and style. You will strive to maintain consistency in language and style throughout the manuscript. You will check for language-related infelicities such as excessive use of the passive voice, misplaced modifiers, and dangling participles. You will fact-check that all real-world details mentioned in the story are correct and consistent. When it comes to fact-checking the fictional elements of a story, a detailed style sheet will come in handy. For the purposes of this chapter, I am assuming you already have basic copyediting skills and so I will talk only about issues that are unique to fiction copyediting.

Let me be frank here. There is no one-approach-fits-all when it comes to copyediting fiction. Editing fiction is creative work, just as writing fiction is. And every editor will have a different method of looking at a manuscript. The method I am outlining here is one that I have worked on for more than seven years. It has taken a different shape today than what I started with, and I am sure I would keep streamlining or improving things as I go on. But I am sharing the method with the hope that you, the reader, would gain something from it that will help you streamline your own approach.

The first pass

The first pass is when I read the manuscript for the first time to get acquainted with the story, characters, and the author's style of writing. I make small notes about anything that jumps out at me, but I am not in a hurry to make style decisions or draft queries at this stage. During the first pass, I am reading to immerse myself in the fictional world the author has created so that I can check if anything throws me off the story. I also notice the level of detail the author has gone into, so I know how much work will be needed on the style sheet.

I am also doing basic clean-up during this read: nothing major that demands author queries, but merely fixing outright errors such as typos, incorrect punctuation, and erratic spacing. I am aware that I may not catch all the glitches during this first pass, and that is okay – because I will be doing the heavy lifting during the second pass when I have a complete picture in front of me. The second pass is also when I will be creating the style sheet that will help me to be consistent within the fictional world.

Creating a style sheet

Just as you would in copyediting non-fiction, feel free to compile a style sheet for fiction manuscripts. If a style sheet is already provided (such as that based on a publisher's house style or a style sheet used for previous books in the series), use it as the base document and build on it. If not, create your own. You can create one from scratch or download a template online. Louise Harnby offers many resources for fiction editors on her website, and a style sheet template is among them.

Early in my career, I picked up a tip regarding style sheets from Amy J Schneider. She posted a series of blog posts wherein she said that she creates four separate style sheets: one each for general style, characters, timelines, and locations. Although I do not go as far as creating four separate style sheets, I do divide my own style sheet template into four sections to note these specifics, and I must say her tip has served me well over the years. Here is a brief description of what goes into each of the four sections of a style sheet.

General

In the general section of the style sheet, note the basics such as punctuation preferences, treatment of numbers, abbreviations, typography, and a special list of made-up words. There is also a miscellaneous part into which goes anything that does not fit anywhere else. In the absence of a house style, feel free to rely on *The Chicago Manual of Style* (CMoS) as a standard guide, but keep in mind that CMoS is mainly aimed at non-fiction whereas the rules for fiction are much more fluid. Hence you should use it only as a guide and not as a hard and fast rulebook.

In the punctuation part of the general section, note the author's preference for the serial comma, use (or avoidance) of the semicolon, ellipsis, etc. Also write down hyphenation preferences, whether to set off words such as 'too', 'either', and 'anyway' with commas, and possessives of names ending in -s. Notice unusual punctuation used in dialogue, for example 'cause or I'mma.

In the part on numbers, note when to spell out numbers and when not to. For example, I leave street names, addresses, telephone numbers (especially emergency numbers such as 911), gun types and calibres, and years as digits. I note down preferences for writing heights (five two or five-feet-two), clothing size (size 16), decades (the eighties or 80s), time (3:30 pm or three thirty), etc.

In the part covering abbreviations, note down the ones that are widely used in the real world and need no explanation, such as TV and GPS. Also note down the ones that may be ambiguous and need explanation. If there are any abbreviations that are made up by the author for their fictional world, note them down along with their meaning.

Record the choices related to typography to indicate thoughts, mouthed dialogues, telepathic conversations, remembered speech, handwritten letters, text messages, etc. This is also a good place to note the treatment of epithets and forms of address (ma'am, darling, Colonel, Doctor, etc.).

Characters

Most editors prefer to list characters on the style sheet alphabetically. However, I have found that grouping them based on their relationships serves me better when it comes to maintaining consistency – another tip I picked up from Amy. I often group characters (including non-human ones such as fictional gods, named or unnamed pets, and magical relics) by their family, friends, co-workers, and fictional army units.

Write the physical descriptions of the characters, their age, characteristics, habits, their positive as well as negative traits, their pet phrases, scars, tattoos, etc. along with the chapter number in which these are described.

Timeline

Track any references to time, whether relative or direct, in this section. Also notice references to weather, seasons, phases of the moon, and events such as the birthdays of characters, school days, weekends, and holidays. Pay attention to logical inconsistencies relating to the passage of time. (Does it really take six hours to travel from Mumbai to Pune by train?)

Some novels have a non-linear timeline. Maybe characters are moving in parallel timelines, or maybe there is some back and forth between the past and the present. There may be flashbacks. Make a note of these, too.

Locations

As with characters, track anything that could lead to a contradiction later. Note down names of physical regions, cities, villages, fictional townships, rivers, lakes, etc. Also note down cardinal directions and distances. Write the description of the interiors including the decor, colour of walls, location of rooms, number of floors, and even exterior features such as gardens, landscaping, and trees outside windows.

Now that you have a detailed style sheet handy and you are copyediting, imagine you have noted a discrepancy. Now what? If it is a minor contradiction, it is probably safe to change and add a query. But if it is something major that is critical to the plot, query the author and suggest solutions if you can.

The second pass: gaffes authors make that a copyeditor should fix

During the second read-through of the manuscript, you also need to pay attention to some common mistakes fiction authors make. I am listing some of these here.

Check for tautologous expressions involving body parts, as in 'He nodded his head' or 'He shrugged his shoulders' or 'She blinked her eyes' – there is no other body part we can nod except the head, nothing we can shrug except the shoulders, and nothing to blink except the eyes.

Be on the lookout for pet phrases, not of a particular character – those go in the style sheet – but of the author. Often, you will notice expressions or actions that an author uses repeatedly. Characters could be raking their fingers through their hair at the drop of a hat, or taking deep or shallow breaths every now and then. Many times, they would let out a breath they did not even know they were holding, or look up from below their eyelashes. Time to call it out with a gentle query.

Fiction is often born from an author's heart. Authors are trying to paint a picture with their words and often use language-related techniques to wax poetic. As copyeditors of fiction we need to check these do not get overpowering and intrusive for the reader in the long run. Keep a check on mixed metaphors, rhymes, alliteration, assonance, etc., and let the author know when something trips you up.

Check for echoes. These are repeated words in proximity to each other that often make the sentence clumsy and throw the reader off the page.

Similar sounding names or names that begin with the same letter can confuse the readers, especially in a full-length novel with many characters. I know siblings have similar sounding names in real life, but it is best to save readers from this confusion. Sometimes, the names of the characters might change midway: Marla can become Maria and James can become John. Be on the lookout for these lapses.

Mixing up action and dialogue tags is a recurring error even experienced authors sometimes make. ("I'm so happy," she smiled. But smiling is an action; you can't smile a sentence.) In some cases, however, the expression could be commonly used and hence the editor might decide to let it stand.

Look out for continuity problems and unintended jumps in action – objects and people dropping into or out of the story without notice or explanation, doors opening when they were already open, a man taking off his shirt twice, a woman going to bed in a saree but waking up in her favourite pyjamas, characters sitting at home in one paragraph and in a bar in the next, etc.

Beware of characters repeating some information in conversations for the benefit of the reader. Nobody talks like that in real life. People do not narrate an incident in excruciating detail, nor should our characters.

Be careful of factual errors that violate the laws of physics or are contrary to how things usually work in the real world. Check for anachronisms, such as objects, events, etc. mentioned in the times earlier to the appearance of such objects in the world (a WhatsApp message, for example, in 2005). Also check historical usage of words to see if using them in the story would be appropriate.

It is not possible to cover in a short chapter everything that copyediting fiction involves, so I will leave you with some resources for further study. Remember that the devil is in the details. Think of the whole situation by imagining yourself in the scene. Play out the action happening on the page in your imagination. Your Spidey sense coupled with your training will go a long way to benefit your career as a fiction editor.

RESOURCES

Tools

Fiction-editing macros by Paul Beverly
Basic housekeeping and clean-up software, such as the File Cleaner in the Editor's Toolkit Plus
Editing-related software geared towards fiction, such as ProWritingAid or Autocrit
Consistency checkers such as PerfectIt

Blogs

Jane Friedman (www.janefriedman.com/blog)
K M Weiland (www.helpingwritersbecomeauthors.com)
Joanna Penn (www.thecreativepenn.com)

Beth Hill (https://theeditorsblog.net)
Louise Harnby (www.louiseharnbyproofreader.com/blog)
Lisa Poisso (www.lisapoisso.com)
Sophie Playle (www.liminalpages.com/blog)
Janice Hardy (http://blog.janicehardy.com/?m=1)
Jami Gold (www.jamigold.com/blog)

Books

The Chicago Guide to Copyediting Fiction by Amy Schneider
The Magic of Fiction by Beth Hill
Line by Line by Claire Kehrwald Cook
Story by Robert McKee
How Not to Write a Novel by Howard Mittelmark
Write to be Published by Nicola Morgan
Understanding Show, Don't Tell by Janice Hardy

REFERENCE

King S. 2000. *On Writing: a memoir of the craft*, p. 212. New York: Scribner. 288 pp.

Dola Basu Singh (dolabsingh@gmail.com) is a fiction editor and an author. She has been helping authors win contracts and publish bestsellers since the year 2015 (www.shiuli.com). Five of her clients have won the Amazon KDP Pen to Publish contest. She lives in Phagwara, Punjab, India, with her family and pets.

CHAPTER 8

Copyediting for Newspapers and Magazines

Reena Singh

Until a few decades ago, if you were looking for opportunities to profitably use your ability to write and edit, you would have naturally turned to journalism as the only viable career option apart from publishing and house journals. Since the turn of the century and with the popularity of the internet, plenty of new options have popped up such as content editing with a website, e-learning and online publishing, and blogging for corporate houses and individuals. However, print and digital media journalism continues to attract youngsters in large numbers. Old stalwarts in this field say a writer's job might be exciting, but a copyeditor's job allows you the freedom to rewrite as well as edit and see your efforts transform the 'copy' (as text is referred to in newspaper offices) to an article.

THE BRIEF: WHAT THE JOB ENTAILS

So, what qualities go into making a good copyeditor in the newspaper and magazine world? First, you need an ability to spot errors quickly, spruce up lacklustre copy, and give it a decided flourish so that it catches the reader's eye. In journalism, time is of the essence. You may have only one chance to read your article or copy, so even as you read an article for the first time, you need to have those grey cells ticking – and multi-tasking – for you have to be editing and rewriting simultaneously. There is no luxury of time in journalism; no time to go over the copy again and again, pruning a word here or adding a word there. In fact, as you read it for the first – and perhaps the last – time, you have got to be rearranging paragraphs if needed and also adding words or lines that make your copy pack a punch, all at the same time. Editing in a newspaper or magazine means plenty of rewriting, so you always need a stock of clever phrases and idioms at hand, while avoiding clichés to spruce up copy.

But mere editing and rewriting skills are not enough. It is important to be aware and well-informed about politics and current events. If you want to be associated with newspapers and magazines as a copyeditor, keep your interest in news, current affairs, and people at an all-time high. The more curious you are, the better an editor you will be. Moreover, on you rests the final responsibility of clearing the copy that is finally going to be published. So, along with checking grammar and language and adding headlines and subheads, you must also remain updated on trends, sports, and political developments to vet facts in the story assigned to you for editing.

And that is why it is said that although there are many commonplace editors everywhere such as those who mark capitals, pick out grammar and spelling errors, and ensure that the copy adheres to the house style, the ones who leave a mark are those who do all this but also have the ability to turn a copy around in a jiffy, use a turn of phrase or word that leaves readers chuckling appreciatively or recoiling in horror as they visualize the scenes or events the writing conjures up. Your editing skills is what makes the reader yearn to read the article quickly and fully.

If you have these qualities in you, you will succeed in the newspaper and magazine world. You will love it from the start for there is never a dull moment in a newspaper office. It is a happening world, peopled with legendary editors and rewrite men and women who race to produce a newspaper day in and day out and seemingly never tire of it.

ADRENALINE-PACKED WORK ENVIRONMENT

It is a world where adrenaline flows all day long and you often sit on the edge of your seat editing copy or thinking up smart headlines. Adrenaline rides high in your blood and no two days are ever alike. Even the routine copy that you edit can be exciting and it is up to you to make each paragraph readable and come alive for your readers. That apart, copyeditors in a newspaper office are trained to weed out words that are repetitive or sentences and phrases that make no new point. Out they go in one fell swoop, as they say. Clichés are out for the same reason. For if you want to hook your reader, you do not want to say the same thing in the same way, day after day.

WHO MAKES UP THE WORKFORCE

All kinds of people are needed in newspaper and magazine offices. There are writers and editors, besides marketing pros who sell advertising space and think up schemes to push up circulation. Marketing experts are always better paid, and editorial staff has to make peace with that for this one fact is never going to change in the newspaper industry.

THE QUALIFICATIONS ONE NEEDS

Now let us get down to brass tacks. How do you get into this world? What are the qualifications you need to be a copyeditor? You need at least a bachelor's degree in any discipline and, of course, a certain way with words, a sharp eye and the ability to spot errors, and extreme attention to detail. Plus, you must be able to spot verbiage and chop the fluff at once. Besides that, you need to be blessed with news sense and must know the pulse of the people. In other words, you need to be blessed with a certain innate curiosity, for it is this that makes a good reporter or editor, which is why you must know exactly what it is that people want to read.

HOW TO GET IN

The recruitment process is different in different newspapers. There is the word-of-mouth route favoured by many organizations, and there are others who get in through the good old internship route that students must follow in their journalism or media courses. The rest, then, is all up to the intern. So, if you do get a chance to begin your internship in a known newspaper or magazine chain, go all out and think up story ideas. Begin with writing something and once the editorial staff knows that you have a way with words, you will be given a chance to edit copy as well.

Schools and institutes of journalism

Most newspaper and media organizations now have their own journalism or media school and once you have secured admission in it, usually after a written test and an interview, they will train you in various aspects of journalism such as feature writing, reporting, and editing, then send you to their various editorial offices to train as an intern.

Once your examination and practical sessions are over at the end of this one-year postgraduate diploma in journalism, you are almost always absorbed within the parent organization.

Alternatively, if you have obtained a journalism degree through a university or an institute, you are free to apply to any newspaper, magazine, or an electronic media house of your choice. Seeking admission into an organization's own journalism school or media course is really the best way of getting into a large group. These courses are run by most newspaper conglomerates and also by media companies such as India Today, Hindustan Times, the Times of India, and Zee Media. Some of these courses also train you for TV journalism, and all TV channels, too, advertise vacancies for writers and editors on their websites where their video content is displayed.

Organizations also advertise when they wish to recruit staff. Most of these vacancies and career opportunities are listed on the organization's website. Most companies will call you for an admission test and interview to assess your suitability for the job once you have sent in your CV.

However, there is no hard and fast rule that you cannot join a newspaper or magazine without a journalism degree or diploma. Sonal Srivastava, a senior assistant editor with the Times of India group, began her career as a teacher and tennis coach in a school in Agra. But her interest in reading and writing propelled her towards journalism and she expressed her desire to work for the Hindustan Times. As she had no prior experience in journalism, Sonal was offered an unpaid internship with the newspaper and after a year of reporting and editing, she finally landed a job with *HT City* as a sports features writer because of her interest in tennis and cricket.

Soon, she was asked to chip in with food features and her career took off. She was then roped in for production work, which meant deciding the placement of stories on the pages, finding pictures and deciding on visuals, and giving intros and headlines, besides editing reports and features to be published in *HT City*, a supplement that is published daily and distributed along with the *Hindustan Times*. She later moved to NDTV's web pages, then joined an India Today group magazine before joining a weekly newspaper brought out by the Times of India group. Although she began as a reporter-cum-feature writer, she found that her experience in copyediting is what helped make her a complete journalist, at home with both writing and editing. She has been a journalist for more than 17 years now and is content with her career graph.

Newspapers need copyeditors from different streams

All kinds of educational backgrounds are needed on newspaper desks. The law graduate, for instance, may handle legal copy, the economics graduate might seek a job with a financial newspaper, and a science graduate may work on technical, scientific, environment-related, and medical articles. Or your forte may be English and you might have a nose for what readers find interesting. Whatever your background, you have got to excel in the English language and know it well to make a successful career as a copyeditor or writer.

Specialized magazines and supplements

If the pace of work in a newspaper office is not your scene, opt for a weekly newspaper or a weekend section of the newspaper. Or you could opt for a news or features magazine that comes out monthly, fortnightly, or weekly on a niche subject such as sports, fashion, cookery, electronics, or music. There are magazines on parenting and real estate and for children too. Here, the pace of work is a little more relaxed, with your schedule picking up as printing deadlines loom. But unlike the daily newspaper, here the writing is more detailed and in-depth and the editing or rewriting even more thorough.

Magazines and weekly sections of daily newspapers, too, cater to different readers. There are supplements on health, fitness, weekend leisure, lifestyle, science and technology, real estate, finance, and sports to mention just a few. A newspaper or magazine mirrors life, and people from different backgrounds blend in well here, the common link being their fluency in the language of the publication.

A DAY IN THE LIFE OF A COPYEDITOR

Here is an example of what is needed in journalism: you may have before you the copy sent in by a reporter or feature writer or even perhaps by a freelancer, and your task is to edit it to make it print-ready. In a shift of eight hours, you will get several such stories and articles, so you have to work at breakneck speed. In a newspaper or magazine, you have space constraints and know beforehand how many words a copy must have. It is best, therefore, to give your writer the word length assigned to the story on the printed page, keeping aside space for visuals, headlines, intro, and captions.

NEWSPAPER EDITING GUIDELINES

The 5 W's (and an 'H')

The introductory paragraph must have in a nutshell all the information you are trying to convey, because there are many readers who will read only the first couple of paragraphs of a story and then move on to scan the rest of the newspaper. Your news must, therefore, be embedded in the first paragraph itself, and answer all the five W's – Who, What, Where, When, and Why – and also the H – How.

Attention to detail

Names need to be double-checked and so must designations and the time and date of the event the writer of the article has written about. So, the emphasis is on checking the information and news while editing, rewriting, or shuffling paragraphs around so that these elements are addressed in the beginning of the report itself.

Fixed format

Since you already know the number of words that can be accommodated on your printed page, you can edit the report accordingly and cut unnecessary words. Use of the active voice and punch lines wherever necessary to hook your readers has already been stressed on at the beginning of this chapter. A crisp, straightforward, conversational style makes for easy reading and facilitates the reader in understanding the news in one go. The exception could be in legal or medical reporting, where the writing needs to be formal and precise, adhering to facts of the case.

A crisp, conversational, and simple style

Although editors work hard at embellishing copy in the publishing world, in newspapers the emphasis is on using simple language that your readers can understand in one quick read. Therefore, the active voice and short sentences that simplify complex ideas are encouraged.

Features editing

Here the writer can be suitably imaginative, if not poetic, and can build up suspense or interest by playing up puns and using imagery to paint a more vivid picture with words. It all depends on the subject that is being written about. Creativity is, therefore, possible in magazines and features supplements rather than in newspapers, and a number of good writers and editors have found immense satisfaction in working for magazines and weekly supplements.

Headline writing

This is a key component of an editor's skill – giving good, catchy, and even whacky headlines that capture the essence of the story and attract the reader's attention. In that sense, the headline should use the active voice as well as indicate what the story is about. If the headline is followed by an introduction that usually carries more details about the article, then you can afford to have an enigmatic headline that will have the reader clamouring to know more – and is finally hooked by the details that the intro gives. A recent headline in *The Telegraph* was eye-catching and was shared extensively on WhatsApp in journalistic groups. It said, 'Snow White and 12 Dwarfs'. This was the headline for a story on a recent cabinet reshuffle in the Modi government and the 12 dwarfs were the 12 ministers who were axed from their portfolios! A brilliant headline, indeed.

House style

Copyeditors working for the print medium usually follow the publication's house style. This also contains technical instructions such as typefaces and their size, apart from guidelines for capitalization besides niggling details such as whether a space or period is used before an initial, use of dashes and abbreviations, and whether the publication uses American or British spelling. The house style lists whether you are to use uppercase or lowercase for designations and entities such as prime minister, government, president, ministries, and other government bodies. There are usually also guidelines on when to use gender-neutral words and on toning down certain sensitive words to describe physical disabilities. For instance, most publications, to protect their readers' sensibilities, ban the use of such words as 'idiot' and 'blind', replacing them, respectively, with terms such as 'mentally challenged' and 'visually impaired' instead.

The house style is usually sacrosanct in most publications, and the copyeditor must know it well and instinctively adhere to the house style as he or she edits copy.

Only a few decades ago, all articles were edited on paper using elaborate proof-correction symbols. However, now in the era of computers, copyeditors work with the 'track changes' feature of a Microsoft Word document. Through track changes, the writer can see the changes made to the original text, and the file automatically records who made what changes to a particular copy at what stage. Once you hover your cursor over the text in red, you can see who edited your work and at what time and date these changes were made. A new copyeditor might find this feature annoying and disturbing but one soon gets used to it. And later, you will come to love the feature and thank God for its existence.

All said and done, copyediting in a newspaper or magazine is deeply satisfying. Unlike editing in a publishing house where books take as long as six months or even a year to be published, newspaper and magazine work is quick, and the article you copyedited today is published tomorrow or within a few weeks. Most journalists say that copyediting is a very satisfying career and often add that they would not ever trade their experience in this field for any other. As I mentioned before, a newspaper office is the one place where there is never a dull moment.

Reena Singh (reeenasingh@gmail.com) has more than 38 years of experience in senior editorial positions in the Times of India group and Genpact. She worked with India's leading spiritual newspaper, *The Speaking Tree*, as well as with *Femina*, *The Times of India*, and *Delhi Times*. She now runs a spiritual and wellness website (yourspositively.com).

CHAPTER 9

Continuing Professional Development of Copyeditors of Technical Documents

Yateendra Joshi

Time was when print commanded credibility: "But it is printed" was often invoked to assert the veracity of a factual statement. This was true only to the extent that the printed matter in question had passed through several filters as it were: copyeditors, compositors, and proofreaders, people trained to spot and fix errors of all kinds, be they factual inaccuracies, inconsistencies, spelling errors, faulty punctuation, or bad typesetting (excessive or miserly spacing between words and bad line breaks such as thin-king for thinking and fun-ding for funding).

However, the explosion of print, driven by PCs, word-processing programs, and desktop printers, which made it possible for the masses to produce print-quality documents, coupled with globalization and instant telecommunication, meant that print was too common, ephemeral, and instantaneous to maintain the authority it once enjoyed. Sloppily copyedited, cursorily spell-checked, and disgracefully typeset documents – they cannot really be called books or periodicals any more – became the norm. Publishers began to do away with in-house copyeditors and increasingly sought cheap labour in distant lands. Fortunately for some publishing professionals and all readers, the pendulum has begun its return journey towards quality, and copyeditors are once more in demand, especially those from distant lands – distant, that is, from the major consuming centres where English is the native language – who can provide value for money, who can take care of not only spelling, grammar, and punctuation but also style, usage, and idiom, and who can do that quickly enough to offer faster turnaround times. The task demands training and practice and patience. This chapter focuses on training to help those copyeditors who wish to train themselves.

The growing demand for copyediting mentioned earlier is mainly for technical and scientific copyediting, which requires familiarity with subject matter in addition to proficiency in English. "The solution turned acidic; its pH value increased from 6.5 to 8.5." To realize that something is amiss, the copyeditor should know that the pH value has to be less than 7 for a solution to be acidic. "The collection of plants comprised 15 genera, spread across 10 species." Again, it is not enough to know that the plural of genus is genera or to wonder whether to use words instead of figures; the copyeditor should spot the anomaly: because each genus comprises one or more species, the number of species cannot be lower than that of genera but must be equal to or greater than that. Although a copyeditor cannot be expected to know as much about a subject as an expert does, she or he should be familiar enough with basic concepts and terminology of a given field, be it archaeology or zoology, to understand the text to be copyedited.

Another requirement is familiarity with the publishing sphere. Although copyeditors typically work on electronic files of word-processed text, it is important for them to know at least a little about the circumstances that led to the file and about its fate once they are done with it. Copyeditors who handle manuscripts of research papers, for instance, should know a little about research, the importance of publishing papers to a scientist's career, and the publication process. Copyeditors who work on book-length jobs should know a bit about how books are produced and marketed, and copyeditors who work for stuff that is published on the web should know at least the rudiments of HTML and how web publishing works.

Aspiring copyeditors, therefore, need to focus on four aspects, namely language, subject matter, style, and production. I will discuss each in turn.

PROFICIENCY IN ENGLISH

To begin with, those who are thinking of making a career in STM (scientific, technical, and medical) copyediting need to have above-average command of English. I suggest that you check your level of proficiency by visiting the Oxford graded readers webpage (https://tinyurl.com/eltouptest). Click on Level 5 or Level 6 and take the two tests. Once you clear Level 6, you can be reasonably confident of your proficiency, although eventually you need to aim at either CAE or CPE in the IELTS suite of examinations (Certificate of Advanced English or Certificate of Proficiency in English).

FAMILIARITY WITH SUBJECT

Copyediting technical texts requires at least some familiarity with the subject matter. It helps to have a degree in biology to copyedit manuscripts dealing with biology; in engineering, to copyedit manuscripts related to engineering; in medicine, to copyedit medical stuff, and so on – provided you are proficient in English, proficient enough, that is, not only to write grammatical English but also to spot and fix errors of grammar and unidiomatic expressions. This is because it is not feasible to teach biology to physicists or to acquire the required proficiency in English grammar and composition on the job. However, it is not too difficult to learn the conventions of style, basic typography, print production, rudiments of HTML, use of Microsoft Word, and so on.

STYLE

In editing and publishing, the term 'style' has a distinct meaning, quite separate from what we may understand by literary style. In the context of this chapter, the word refers to thousands of totally trivial decisions that need to be made when a given text is to be formally published. For example, should it be the Second World War or World War 2? Health care or Healthcare? Dept. (with the dot) or Dept (without the dot)? When are numbers to be spelt out (twelve or 12)? Compilations of such decisions are referred to as style guides or style manuals. Familiarity with one or more of these compilations is a copyeditor's bread and butter. If you wish to take up copyediting as a career, you must become thoroughly familiar with the style guides commonly used in your chosen field and region (e.g. *The Chicago Manual of Style* or the *New Oxford Style Manual* or *The Economist Style Guide*).

PRODUCTION

Copyediting is one part of the process through which raw text becomes a published piece of work, whether paper-based or electronic. Familiarity with production is what sets novice copyeditors apart from expert copyeditors. Fortunately, such familiarity is not difficult to acquire. Web designers, graphic artists, printers, paper merchants, IT professionals . . . all are usually happy to explain their craft to enthusiastic learners. But that does mean leaving the comforts of your desk! I recall how the staff of the Publications and Information Directorate of the Council of Scientific and Industrial Research were happy to accept trainee copyeditors from TERI's Publications Unit and introduce them to print production. (The Energy and Resources Institute, New Delhi, is better known simply as TERI.)

Now that we know what is required, we can discuss how to go about acquiring these skills and the relevant knowledge.

WAYS TO SHARPEN YOUR SKILLS AS A COPYEDITOR

Comparing manuscripts before and after copyediting

Formal training is necessarily analytical; it focuses on one aspect at a time: grammar or style or formatting, for example. However, 'in the trenches', copyeditors handle these aspects simultaneously, and a useful way to orient trainee copyeditors is to ask them to compare the original and the copyedited versions of a manuscript. Such a comparison is easier to make when copyeditors work on hard copy or printouts, and trainees can compare the marked-up copy with the revised printout. When copyeditors work on soft copies, the changes are recorded using the 'track changes' feature of Microsoft Word and can be made visible selectively. A heavily copyedited file can look even more intimidating when viewed in this mode. The solution is to make the changes visible selectively, focusing in turn on comments, formatting, and insertions and deletions. Another approach is to print out the original file and its revised version after accepting all the changes. Although some may consider this a waste of paper, the method is more conducive to learning and may be more cost effective if the editors' time is also taken into account besides material resources such as paper and toner.

Looking at archives of Copyediting-L

Copyediting-L (http://www.copyediting-l.info/) is an electronic discussion group of about 1500 copyeditors the world over (but mostly from the United States) "for copyeditors and other defenders of the English language who want to discuss anything related to editing" from tricky points of style to philosophical aspects, from submitting a quote to ensuring that they are paid, and from the latest electronic tools to finding out-of-print books. Because the group is very active (dozens of messages every day), it is counterproductive to read the messages as they come in or even as 'digests', which are not actually digests but aggregates (many individual messages, up to about 500 lines, combined into one large message with a table of contents). A better strategy is to subscribe to the list but choose not to receive any message from the list, log on to the archives two or three times a week – it is training after all – and scan the weekly aggregates for topics that appear relevant or interesting. The messages are tagged: the tag Usage, for example, deals with grammar and style issues; Query deals with questions not related to grammar and style; and Tools covers messages related to hardware and software, books, websites, and anything else a copyeditor might need (including desks and pencils and magnifiers). A similar group, not as active but one largely devoted to science, is the EASE Forum, run by the European Association of Science Editors.

The Chartered Institute of Editing and Proofreading, in the United Kingdom, also runs a similar platform, but it is open only to members (https://www.ciep.uk/resources/forums/about).

Working as an intern at a research institute

Copyediting is above all a solitary occupation: while working on a manuscript, nothing else exists for the copyeditor apart from the file, a few reference books, and perhaps the internet for quick look-ups. It is all the more important, therefore, for trainee copyeditors to see their work in context, to be aware of their role in the publishing sphere mentioned above. For copyeditors who work on research papers, it is a salutary experience to work alongside researchers, to see at first hand the instruments and the procedures mentioned in the Methods section of research papers, to visit experimental sites, and to understand why publishing is crucial to a scientist's career. Most research institutes will welcome trainee copyeditors if they volunteer to copyedit a paper or two during their internship. To cite a specific instance, I recall that the National Chemical Laboratory in Pune had welcomed such an intern from Cactus Communications. The idea of working as an intern could be extended, for example, to visiting a printing press, a typesetting bureau, a book bindery, and so on.

Reading well-crafted prose

A good copyeditor is also a competent writer, someone who can craft at least a few sentences of lucid prose when the occasion demands. Although preserving the voice of the writer is often considered important, it is seldom so with research papers written by people who do not have English as their first language: these writers are far more concerned about getting their paper accepted by a reputable journal than about the niceties of their prose style, if they have one to begin with. Copyediting very poorly written papers will need you to go well beyond fixing the grammar but without turning the task into substantive editing. A simple and practical way to tell the two apart is the level of changes: copyediting rarely changes the original order of sentences, let alone that of paragraphs; substantive editing usually involves large-scale rearrangement of text. But if the copyeditor is to re-write a sentence, she or he must be a competent writer. And massive exposure to good writing is one of the most effective ways to improve one's writing. For copyeditors, exposure to badly written prose is an occupational hazard; an antidote is therefore essential and can take the form of reading quality prose (e.g. winners of the annual Royal Society Prize for Science Books and that featured in the two annual anthologies, namely the *Best American Science Writing*, now discontinued, and the *Best American Nature and Science Writing*). Reading is a time-intensive activity, and it is essential to build some time for such reading into a copyeditor's schedule.

Copyeditors should also keep up with their field by reading, or at least being aware of, the latest books, newsletters, and blogs relevant to the profession: revised editions of standard style and usage guides, newsletters such as *Science Editor* (published monthly by the Council of

Science Editors), *European Science Editing* (published by the European Association of Science Editors), and *Tracking Changes* (published four times a year by ACES: The Society for Editing), and blogs such as The Slot (http://theslot.blogspot.com/).

Copyediting is neither glamorous nor exciting. But it can be a rewarding profession if you are passionate about language, an avid reader, and a lifelong learner.

Yateendra Joshi (yateendra.joshi@gmail.com) has been copyediting scientific and technical texts for nearly 35 years, a career switch he made after working for a decade as an agricultural scientist. In 2014, he was recognized as a master editor by BELS, the Board of Editors in Life Sciences, USA (as of 2022, only 30 editors worldwide have earned this distinction). Yateendra is a member of the council of EASE, the European Association of Science Editors; a member-at-large of the board of directors, BELS; and a member of the editorial board of *Information Design Journal*. He holds a master's degree in agriculture and a Certificate in Advanced English (IELTS). Yateendra regularly conducts training programmes for researchers and academics on how to write, publish, and present.

PART III

Technique and Craft

CHAPTER 10

Grammar Notes

A Brief Guide to Logical and Clear Writing

Ellen Sue Feld

The smallest things can create ambiguity, and ambiguity can lead to big misunderstandings. How we interpret text affects our approach to editing it. Part of our goal as editors is to ensure that writers say what they mean and intend what they say. In this chapter, I explore ways to make writing structurally sound, clear, and logical.

Key terms

- structural shifts
- syntax and modifiers
- faulty reference
- diction and logic

STRUCTURAL SHIFTS

Have you ever understood what a sentence intends to say while at the same time sensed something was not quite right? A sentence that seems illogical or somehow wrong may be a mixed construction or an incomplete comparison.

These structural problems result when sentence parts do not successfully work together. You can resolve structural shifts by following a few rules.

Mixed constructions

A mixed construction occurs when two parts of a sentence – subject/predicate or subject/complement – do not logically connect.

To fix these mixed constructions, we need to change or add some words.

Illogical subjects

Subjects can be illogical because they are located where they do not belong:

- inside prepositional phrases
- inside clauses beginning with subordinating conjunctions

Here is a prepositional phrase that is an illogical subject:

> In the very early, dark morning hours helps students memorize crucial points while they are preparing for oral exams.

In this sentence, the true subject is in the prepositional phrase 'In the very early, dark morning hours'.

However, the rules of good grammar say that the subject of a sentence cannot reside in a prepositional phrase. To make a logical subject, you need to remove it from the prepositional phrase.

You probably understand that the sentence means the following:

> The very early, dark morning hours can be an ideal time for students to memorize crucial points while preparing for oral exams.

Now the sentence has a real and logical subject. (Notice that when you eliminate the preposition, you may also have to make small adjustments to the rest of the sentence.)

Here are a couple of examples of subordinate clauses (also known as dependent clauses) as illogical subjects:

> Although I wanted to go wasn't enough of a reason.
>
> Because the bus ride was so long, bumpy, and hot made students feel sick upon returning to the classroom.

Are you able to find the true subject of each sentence? Each subject is buried within the clause that begins with a subordinating conjunction.

Let us free each subject from its clause and rewrite the sentences. Logical possibilities are these.

> I wanted to go, but that wasn't enough of a reason.
>
> The long, bumpy, hot bus ride made students feel sick upon returning to the classroom.

Illogical predicates

The rules of good grammar also tell us that the predicate of a sentence cannot be in a subordinate clause.

Here is an example of an illogical predicate:

> The number of high school students who don't get enough sleep, which is on the rise due to earlier school start times.

You will find the true predicate within the dependent clause beginning with the word 'which'.

A sentence such as this is easy to correct. You can free the predicate by removing the word that makes the clause dependent:

> The number of high school students who don't get enough sleep is on the rise due to earlier school start times.

Illogical complements

First, a quick refresher: a complement follows a linking verb. Complements 'equal' their subjects. Complements are nouns or adjectives.

Here is an example of a logical complement:

> She is nice.

Here is an example of an illogical complement:

> The health problems that result because young children are going to bed later and getting up earlier are when paediatricians get motivated to issue guidelines for healthier sleep habits.

What is wrong with this sentence? It tells us that the health problems 'are when'. But 'when' – an adverb – cannot be a complement.

You can correct this sentence with different approaches. You could adjust the subject, adjust the complement, or rewrite the sentence.

Here is a suggestion:

> The health problems that result because young children are going to bed later and getting up earlier motivate paediatricians to issue guidelines for healthier sleep habits.

You can solve the problem by removing the linking verb 'are' and the adverb 'when' and replacing them with the action verb 'motivate'.

Incomplete comparisons

Complete comparisons must be grammatically parallel. Like a scale with two pans, to achieve balance, a complete comparison requires equally weighted elements at both ends of the sentence.

An incomplete comparison results when something is missing from what should be parallel parts of a sentence. Here is an example:

> He appreciates fiction books more than most of his friends.

We begin to wonder what is being compared to what. The sentence could mean either of the following:

> He appreciates fiction books more than he appreciates most of his friends.

> He appreciates fiction books more than most of his friends do.

The logical solution (the second sentence) is that his appreciation of fiction books is being compared to his friends' appreciation of fiction books. Therefore, the sentence needs to make clear that 'he' and 'his friends' are parallel, each in the same subject–verb format: he appreciates/his friends do.

Faulty comparisons usually omit words or contain words in the wrong form. You can correct faulty comparisons by adding the necessary words or changing word forms.

SYNTAX AND MODIFIERS

Syntax (or word order) affects meaning. Syntax problems can result in sentences that are funny or ridiculous at best and ambiguous or confusing at worst.

Modifiers are some of the chief culprits in problems involving word order. A modifier can be a single word, such as an adjective or adverb, or it can be a group of words, such as a phrase or clause. Likewise, a modifier can describe a single word, such as a verb, or a group of words, such as a phrase.

We will focus on the placement of modifiers and the effect of placement on meaning.

Syntax and meaning

To show the effect of syntax on meaning, we will start with two sentences that are grammatically and logically sound. The sentences contain identical words, but differ in word order and in the placement of the comma.

> We looked out to the horizon hopefully, praying that the lost ship would soon appear.

> We looked out to the horizon, praying hopefully that the lost ship would soon appear.

Meaning changes according to the placement of one word. In the first sentence, the adverb 'hopefully' is working with the verb 'looked'. We are, therefore, looking out to the horizon with hope. In the second sentence, 'hopefully' is working with the verb 'praying'. Now we are praying with hope. Both sentences work successfully even though their meanings are different.

Now let us look at some other example sentences to see what makes them confusing or wrong.

Misplaced modifiers

Misplaced modifiers, as their name indicates, are in the wrong place. They end up describing the wrong thing:

> The little boy was hungry and wanted to eat his peanut butter and jelly sandwich, so he quickly pedalled his bike back home ravenously.

At a glance, we understand what this sentence likely means:

> The little boy quickly pedalled his bike home because he was ravenous and wanted to eat his sandwich.

The sentence means to tell us that the boy was 'ravenously hungry', but it tells us that he 'pedalled ravenously'.

Let us change the word order to reflect the intended meaning:

> The little boy was ravenously hungry and wanted to eat his peanut butter and jelly sandwich, so he quickly pedalled home.

To create clear text, we place modifiers as close as possible to the word or words they are intended to describe.

Dangling modifiers

Dangling modifiers are dangling because they have nothing to modify: the person or thing they are intended to describe is missing from the sentence. It is easy, therefore, for a reader to relate the modifier to the next closest word. This leads to a confusing and sometimes humorous sentence that lacks logic:

> After wandering around lost for hours on the hiking path, our backpacks felt heavier and heavier.

It seems as if the modifying phrase 'after wandering around lost for hours on the hiking path' is modifying the sentence subject 'backpacks'. Logic tells us, though, that the backpacks are not wandering around lost.

You can fix the dangling modifier by rewriting the sentence to include what was missing.

Here are two possible approaches:

> After wandering around lost for hours on the hiking path, we felt as if our backpacks were getting heavier and heavier.

> After we had been wandering around lost for hours on the hiking path, our backpacks felt heavier and heavier.

Ambiguous modifiers

Sometimes, a modifier simultaneously describes two things in a sentence. This act of double duty results in ambiguous meaning.

Here is an example of an ambiguous modifier:

> Film reviewers who write forcefully sway the movie-going audience.

The word 'forcefully' is a modifier that could be describing the verb 'write' or the verb 'sway'.

First you must decide what the modifier is modifying. Then, to end the ambiguity, you may have to revise the sentence.

Here are two possibilities:

> Reviewers who write forcefully can sway the movie-going audience.

> Reviewers who write forceful articles sway the movie-going audience.

FAULTY REFERENCE

Faulty reference occurs when a pronoun does not have a clear antecedent (or referent) or lacks one altogether. We will look at two types of faulty reference:

- ambiguous pronouns
- dangling pronouns.

Ambiguous pronouns

Pronouns can be ambiguous just as modifiers can. An ambiguous pronoun has two or more possible antecedents. Here are two examples:

> The girl asked her mother if she would be home in time to watch their favourite show.

> I asked for a short stack of whole wheat pancakes topped with blueberries but got two cold plates with one pancake on each, with blueberries in a side dish, which is not my preference.

In the first sentence, we are not sure if the pronoun 'she' refers to 'girl' or to 'mother'. In the second sentence, we are not sure if the relative pronoun clause – 'which is not my preference' – refers to one, all, or any combination of the ways in which the pancakes and blueberries were served.

Fixing ambiguous pronouns

There is more than one way to fix a sentence with an ambiguous pronoun. But before you revise, you need to analyse. Let us work on the first example sentence:

> The girl asked her mother if she would be home in time to watch their favourite show.

Step one: Determine what the sentence is supposed to mean.
If the word 'mother' is the antecedent, the sentence means

> The girl asked if her mother would be home in time to watch their favourite show.

If the word 'girl' is the antecedent, the sentence means

> The girl wanted to know if she would be home in time to watch their favourite show.

Step two: Revise the sentence to make the antecedent clear. Let us suppose that the word 'mother' is the antecedent:

> The girl asked her mother if her mother would be home in time to watch their favourite show.

This solution, while clarifying the antecedent, is also repetitive and dull. Rewriting with a direct quotation is one way to eliminate these drawbacks:

> The girl asked her mother, "Will you be home in time to watch our favourite show?"

If the word 'girl' is the antecedent, the sentence could read as follows:

> The girl asked her mother, "Will I be home in time to watch our favourite show?"

Let's revise the second example:

> I asked for a short stack of whole wheat pancakes topped with blueberries but got two cold plates with one pancake on each, with blueberries and whipped cream in a side dish, which is not my preference.

Here are two possible rewrites:

> I asked for a short stack of whole wheat pancakes topped with blueberries but got two cold plates with one pancake on each, with blueberries in a side dish. Cold plates and blueberries on the side aren't my preferences.

> I asked for a short stack of whole wheat pancakes topped with blueberries but got two cold plates with one pancake on each, with blueberries in a side dish. My breakfast wasn't served the way I wanted it.

Dangling pronouns

A dangling pronoun lacks an antecedent much in the same way that a dangling modifier lacks something to describe:

> When he looked back on his education, he realized that he never took any courses in psychology, yet he still wished he could be one.

The pronoun 'one' has no antecedent. Did 'he' wish that he could be 'courses in psychology'? That interpretation does not make sense.

It is easy to create a faulty reference. We might have all the details worked out in our minds but not in our writing. We understand what we mean to say, but our readers may not.

Fixing dangling pronouns

To fix a sentence with a missing antecedent, first determine what the missing antecedent should be. Then rewrite to supply the antecedent.

Here is the problem sentence again:

> When he looked back on his education, he realized that he never took any courses in psychology, yet he still wished he could be one.

To establish the missing sentence element, we want to answer this question: What does he wish he could be? One logical answer is 'psychologist'.

Here is a suggested rewrite:

> When he looked back on his education, he realized that he never took any courses in psychology, yet he still wished he could be a psychologist.

DICTION AND LOGIC

Occasionally, a sentence can demonstrate good grammar but use the wrong words. Or a sentence might have all the right grammatical ingredients but be illogical nonetheless.

Diction

'Diction' is word choice. Informal writing calls for informal diction, and formal writing calls for formal diction. That sounds straightforward, but there are many shades of diction: academic, scientific, highfalutin, colloquial, and poetic, to name a few. Scientific writing, for example, belongs in text designed for scientists, not in a general information blog for laypeople. The wrong diction can alienate a reader.

When we are looking for word options to create variety and avoid repetition, a thesaurus can be a wonderful tool. This same tool can land us on a word choice that is inappropriate, pompous, or silly.

It is important to know how to use a word within the context of a particular piece of writing. When you work with a thesaurus and find new words to replace the words you are accustomed to using, it is easy to select words that are not right in the context of a particular text.

Compare the sentences in the two pairs below. Notice how the appropriate word choice in the second sentence of each pair has the bonus of making the writing more concise.

Pair 1

> The girl was felicitous upon receiving her allowance.
> The girl was happy to get her allowance.

Pair 2

> I desire the opportunity to proffer my prize daffodils at the floral convention.
> I would like to present my prize daffodils at the flower show.

Logic

Some sentences do not make sense even if all the grammatical elements are in place.

Consider this sentence:

> My goal for the summer is to try and put an end to people who do experiments on animals when they could be using a computer.

That sentence sounds threatening, and it is confusing. Its literal meaning is quite different from its intended meaning. It says:

> My goal for the summer is to kill people who prefer doing experiments on animals rather than spending their time working on computers.

This interpretation almost certainly does not match the writer's intention. Here is a possible rewrite:

> My goal for the summer is to try to put an end to vivisection when researchers could instead be using a computer to conduct their studies.

Being aware of diction and logic can work wonders when you edit. Before creating a final draft, try reading the text aloud and ask yourself:

- Does the language fit the subject matter and the reading audience?
- Does it make good, plain sense?

A 'Yes' to both questions means you are on target; a 'No' to one or both questions indicates you have some editing to do.

SUMMING IT ALL UP

When we edit, we sometimes need to go beyond the rules for concrete grammatical elements such as punctuation, tense, and possessives. We may need to use our ability to understand and intuit what a writer intends and watch for mismatched structures, the order of words and phrases as they affect meaning, missing elements, reference problems, and the appropriate level of language. We may also need to use a little creativity and finesse to solve problems of clarity and logic as we transform ambiguous writing into smooth, sensible text.

Ellen Sue Feld (ellen@grammar-lion.com) has been a reporter, a copy chief, an essayist, a website reviewer, and a developmental editor. She earned her MA in Writing from Johns Hopkins University and is the author of *Comma Sense: your guide to grammar victory* and the children's book *Paragon and Jubilee*. Her online grammar refresher courses (grammar-lion.com) have served more than 45,000 students.

CHAPTER 11

House Style, Style Guides, and Style Manuals

Yateendra Joshi

The word 'house' in house style presumably refers to a publishing house, and 'style' is a compilation of preferences in matters related to rendering words into print (not necessarily on paper, though). Taken one at a time, these matters are often trivial; for example, is it make-up or makeup? 5 km/h or 5 km h^{-1} or 5 kmph? In a numbered list, should each number be followed by a dot? It is not as though only one option is the correct one each time – it is simply a matter of what a publishing house prefers. And through hundreds of such preferences arises a house style, with the compilations getting longer with every new edition. *The Chicago Manual of Style* ran to 200 pages in its first edition: the current (17th) edition runs to 1144. To be precise, the first 12 editions were simply titled *Manual of Style*; 'Chicago' and the definite article were added from the 13th edition.

'Style guide' and 'style manual' are used interchangeably, although the former is more common in the United Kingdom (*The Times Style Guide*, for example) and the latter, in the United States (*The New York*

Times Manual of Style and Usage, for example), whereas 'stylebook' is usually associated with newspapers in the United States.

The word 'style' itself has several meanings, best captured by Cochran (1978), who lists four kinds of style: (1) editorial, (2) typographic, (3) literary, and (4) usage. In the context of this chapter, most style guides cover the first two: editorial style refers to abbreviations, capitalization, punctuation, and so on, or matters of consistency, and typographic style refers to italics and boldface and small capitals, spaces, dashes, and so on, or matters related to typesetting.

TOPICS COVERED BY STYLE GUIDES

Style guides are compiled to meet the needs of a publishing house or other organizations that publish a great deal. Some of the more comprehensive compilations or those from prestigious publishing houses are adopted by other publishers or other organizations. As with dictionaries, it is also common to nominate one guide as 'default': "Follow it unless stated otherwise", with a smaller, bespoke compilation covering only the exceptions and matters not covered by the default guide. This is understandable, because the published content can range from novels – which are relatively straightforward in terms of typography – to comprehensive textbooks, field guides, and handbooks. Major newspapers, for example, require guidance on how to spell names of people and places from the world over, whereas a publisher of books on physics has little need for such information but needs clear guidance on Greek letters, mathematical symbols, equations, and so on.

Style guides also vary in the depth to which they cover topics related to grammar and usage, but all cover the more mechanical aspects related to typesetting and, increasingly, coding. One way to think about this difference between the two kinds of style guides – those that cover grammar and usage and those that do not – is to imagine what would be needed if the content were to be in manuscript or typescript alone, that is either written out in longhand on paper or produced using a manual typewriter. In one stroke, this removes such matters as italics and boldface, en dashes and em dashes, all sorts of spaces, and special characters such as diacritical marks and Greek letters. However, guidance will yet be necessary in terms of capitalization, hyphenation, and punctuation, for example.

WHY USE STYLE GUIDES

Style guides are professional tools – best left alone if the job in hand does not call for professional standards (jobs that are too small, ephemeral, or informal) or if your focus is only on improving expression and eliminating errors related to grammar and usage or if you cannot spare the time for putting finishing touches. In any case, tools such as PerfectIt can catch many of the inconsistencies. Remember, a style guide is for polishing, for putting finishing touches, not for creating or building. Style guides are for those who obsess over small matters, although it is good to remember what Carey (1958) said: "The mind of one who happens to have an eye for a comma is not necessarily incapable of comprehending larger issues or embracing wider interests."

However, you may want to, or be compelled to, refer to a style guide because your author may want you to or because you wish to impress fellow copyeditors (especially those who make hiring decisions) or to settle arguments and save time or merely out of a desire to do a professional job.

HOW TO USE STYLE GUIDES

Style guides are professional tools. As with any other professional tool, it is near-impossible to master their use in a single sitting. It is only through continued use that one can become familiar with a given guide, learning, over time, what the guide covers (and, equally important, what it does not), where to find that nugget of information you are looking for (Is it 4.00 p.m. or 4:00 p.m. or 4 PM or 4 PM or 4 pm or 1600 hours . . .?), and whether its recommendations have changed over time. This is possible if you are willing to leaf through your chosen style guide every now and then – not because the job in hand requires such consultation but merely to become more familiar with the tool.

Remember that different style guides may offer different answers: for example, it is only in its 11th edition that the *AMA Manual of Style* joined most other guides in inserting a space between the value and symbol in giving temperature (29 °C; not 29°C anymore), although it continues to dispense with the dot in 'et al.', recommending that it should be 'et al' instead.

WHICH STYLE GUIDE TO USE

The choice will be dictated largely by the subject domain and the customer's preference and to some extent by the country or region. Probably the most widely used and preferred across the board is *The Chicago Manual of Style*. If you copyedit exclusively in medicine, you will most probably use the *AMA Manual of Style*. In the social sciences, the *Publication Manual of the American Psychological Association* (currently in its 7th edition) is the style guide most commonly used, whereas in the humanities, it is probably the *MLA Handbook* (currently in its 8th edition, published by the Modern Language Association). Then there are the *Microsoft Manual of Style*, the *Yahoo! Style Guide*, and so on. For those who copyedit scientific stuff, there is *Scientific Style and Format*, the most comprehensive in terms of the disciplines covered (now in its 8th edition but a new one expected in 2023), the *Science Editors' Handbook*, and even the *New Oxford Dictionary for Scientific Writers and Editors*. If you edit in chemistry, the style guide by the American Chemical Society – the

ACS Guide to Scholarly Communication – may be the one you want (available on subscription, online only). As you can see, the list is seemingly endless even without such stalwarts as the *New Oxford Style Manual* and *Butcher's Copy-editing*, which cover the preferences of the Oxford University Press and the Cambridge University Press, respectively.

FINDING ANSWERS WHEN A STYLE GUIDE DOES NOT OFFER THEM

No style guide can be expected to answer every question about style or usage. If your go-to guide offers no help, consult another and then some more; visit https://www.chicagomanualofstyle.org/qanda/latest.html and see if the question has been answered; or post your question to Copyediting-L or to the EASE Forum or to the forum – although open only to members of the CIEP – run by the Chartered Institute of Editing and Proofreading. For APA style, check the blog available at https://apastyle.apa.org/blog.

Lastly, be aware that style guides, which exist mainly to ensure consistency, are particularly liable to be replaced with automated tools, PerfectIt being a good example. All the more reason for copyeditors to keep sharpening their other skills: the ability to rephrase where required, to query faulty logic, to make tables more user-friendly, and so on.

REFERENCES

Carey G V. 1958. *Mind the Stop: a brief guide to punctuation*, p. 10. Harmondsworth, UK: Penguin Books. 126 pp.

Cochran W. 1978. Four kinds of style, pp. 341–346 in *Scientific Information Transfer: the editor's role*, edited by M Balaban. Dordrecht: D. Reidel. 686 pp. [Proceedings of the First International Conference of Scientific Editors, Jerusalem, 24–29 April 1977]

Yateendra Joshi (yateendra.joshi@gmail.com) has been copyediting scientific and technical texts for nearly 35 years, a career switch he made after working for a decade as an agricultural scientist. In 2014, he was recognized as a master editor by BELS, the Board of Editors in Life Sciences, USA (as of 2022, only 30 editors worldwide have earned this distinction). Yateendra is a member of the council of EASE, the European Association of Science Editors; a member-at-large of the board of directors, BELS; and a member of the editorial board of *Information Design Journal.* He holds a master's degree in agriculture and a Certificate in Advanced English (IELTS). Yateendra regularly conducts training programmes for researchers and academics on how to write, publish, and present.

CHAPTER 12

How to Write Effective Queries to Authors

Divya Jyoti Munjal

Querying is an important part of the editorial process because it serves as the primary means of communication between the author and the copyeditor, the foundation of a productive working partnership, and a useful record of decisions taken for future reference. 'Author queries' – short for queries to the author – require authors' active engagement in making their manuscript fit for publication.

By raising author queries, a copyeditor can obtain the information needed for polishing the manuscript. However, writing author queries is an art in which every copyeditor needs to be proficient. Firstly, the copyeditor should be able to be in the shoes of the reader and look for anything that could detract from usefulness and accuracy of the final product. Secondly, the copyeditor should be able to frame queries that are polite, clear, and concise.

Before starting any editing job, an efficient copyeditor conducts some basic analysis of the input material. This analysis helps him or her to get an idea about the kind of queries that need to be raised while editing the manuscript.

The copyeditor decides what not to query, drawing on the acquired skills and expertise to make minor changes or corrections to spelling, grammar, punctuation, and so on.

WHOM TO QUERY: AUTHOR OR PROJECT MANAGER?

A copyeditor may receive editing assignments from a publisher through a project manager or directly from an author. Some queries should be addressed to the project manager and some to the author. Whom to query depends upon the kind of query.

Queries to be raised with the project manager

If the copyeditor comes across a manuscript that follows a style that is completely different from the standard guidelines specified for that job, the matter should be raised with the project manager. For example, if the author–date format has been specified for citations, but the manuscript uses numbered citations, or vice versa, the copyeditor should ask the project manager whether to change the format of the citations or leave them as they are. The initial analysis helps in dealing with such matters early on to avoid delays in the publishing schedule.

Queries to be raised with authors

Queries related to the following matters should be taken up with the author: missing data or discrepancies in data, incomplete or ambiguous sentences, and missing elements or parts including references, citations, figures and tables, and references to them in the text. Queries should also be raised to ascertain that any changes made to the content are acceptable to authors because, after all, it is their content and they know more about it than anyone else.

Similarly, in the case of missing bibliographic details in references, the copyeditor should ascertain whether supplying the missing details is part of the copyediting service. (References are covered later in the chapter.)

The rest of the chapter deals with queries to the author.

IMPORTANT POINTS TO BE KEPT IN MIND WHILE QUERYING AUTHORS

- Maintain a polite, professional, and constructive tone. Using polite expressions such as 'please' and 'thanks' helps to build rapport with the author and thereby helps to obtain the required clarification from the author.
- If any sentence is unclear, either rephrase the sentence (and ask the author to verify the change) or reproduce the unclear part of the sentence (and ask the author to check and modify the sentence).
- Keep the queries polite, clear, and concise.
- If possible, suggest an alternative instead of merely querying: for example, highlight the ambiguous 'this' and ask whether the author means A or B to be the antecedent noun.
- Ensure that your queries are grammatically correct.

SAMPLE AUTHOR QUERIES FOR DIFFERENT PARTS OF A MANUSCRIPT

Here are some sample author queries (AQs) related to different parts of a manuscript. In most cases, the manuscript is assumed to be an article meant for an academic journal.

Title

Because the title of an article or a chapter is a crucial part of the manuscript, even a minor change in the title should be queried to seek the author's approval.

> **AQ** The title of the article has been slightly modified to meet the target journal's specifications. Please confirm if the revised title is fine.

Affiliation

For any published material, the affiliation of the author should always be complete. Research papers typically publish these details, and the affiliation comprises the name and address of the institution where the research was carried out – which may be different from the author's current affiliation. Query the author in case of incomplete or missing affiliation.

> **AQ** Please provide the name and full address of the place where the work reported in the manuscript was carried out.

Corresponding authors

Sometimes, details about the manuscript and its author(s) are given on a separate page, referred to as the cover sheet or the title page in the case of research manuscripts. In addition to the information on the affiliations of different authors and some information on the contents (e.g. the number of words, figures, and tables), the page identifies the 'corresponding' author(s) responsible for responding to any queries concerning the manuscript. Query the author if the address for correspondence is missing or is incomplete or if the name of the corresponding author on the title page and on the cover sheet is different.

> **AQ** Please provide the full mailing address including the email address of the corresponding author.

Missing keywords

Keywords are useful to indexers and those searching for information on the subject of the manuscript and often appear after the abstract in manuscripts of research papers. Good keywords are concrete and specific, not too broad, and ideally other than those included in the title of the manuscript because words in the title are indexed by default. Also, a keyword does not have to be a single word (in fact, single words usually make poor keywords). A query is required if keywords are not supplied or are inadequate.

> **AQ** Please provide three to five important keywords relevant to the content.

Abbreviations

If the author repeatedly uses an abbreviation but has failed to spell it out or explain it, and the copyeditor is either unable to find the expanded form or unsure of it, a query is required.

> **AQ** Please spell out 'ABC' in full: do you mean Australian Broadcasting Corporation?

Always keep in mind that identical abbreviations may represent totally different things, and the copyeditor should not insert the spelt-out version without querying the author (e.g. IFS may stand for Indian Foreign Service, Indian Forest Service, or even Irish Free State). If the copyeditor can find the expanded form, it should be inserted at the first occurrence of the term and the author requested to confirm that the spelt-out version is correct.

> **AQ** Please check whether 'IFS' stands for Indian Foreign Service.

An author using the same abbreviation for different entities should be alerted to the fact.

> **AQ** 'PCB' has been used to mean both 'pentachlorobenzene' and 'printed circuit boards'. Please confirm the appropriate term.

Facts

Errors or discrepancies related to facts should be brought to the attention of the author.

> **AQ** The year mentioned here does not seem to be correct, as this principle was already put forth by XYZ in 1982. Please check and revise as needed.

AQ This idea was not proposed by XYZ, as mentioned in the text. Please check and revise as needed. (Was the idea proposed by ABC?)

Political biases

If the copyeditor feels that the text is biased towards any political party, the author should be requested to make changes to the text to fix the issue.

AQ This statement may lead readers to believe that you are biased. Please rephrase the text so that it does not seem aligned to any political party.

Unclear, ambiguous, or incomplete sentences

If sense is unclear or ambiguous in a given sentence, ask for clarification.

AQ The meaning is unclear in the following sentence: 'After start of infection occurs, a storm ... pulmonary intravascular coagulopathy'. Please rephrase to make the sense clear to readers.

If you have edited the sentence to make the sense clear, please ask if the rephrasing is correct.

AQ Please check if the changes made to the following sentence convey the intended meaning: 'Infection occurs when pathogens attack your body and begin to multiply'.

If any sentence is incomplete or some information seems to be missing in the sentence, query the author.

AQ Please check the following sentence for missing data: 'This is a fact...agree to it'.

If the text explains the impact of a new term but the term has not been introduced earlier, query the author.

AQ This paragraph explains the impact of the term 'circular economy'; however, this term has not been introduced and explained earlier. Please introduce the term before explaining its impact on the study group.

If any words and expressions are being used without any explanation, request the author for additional text.

AQ The meaning of the expression 'usufructuary rights' is not clear. Please add some text to explain the expression to make it easier for your readers.

Missing tables or figures

Every table and figure should have a citation (be mentioned in the text), and every first mention of a table or figure should be accompanied by the corresponding table or figure. If any table or figure is missing, alert the author and ask to provide the missing item. Such lapses are not uncommon in research papers that have been extensively revised to address the comments made by the reviewers of the paper: often, reviewers suggest authors to delete an existing table or figure or to insert a table or figure to strengthen the argument being made in the text.

AQ The text mentions Table 4 on page X, but the corresponding table is missing. Please provide the table.

Missing links or footnotes

Some items within a table or a figure may also be missing, such as a footnote without a matching callout in the text or a callout without a footnote. The copyeditor should bring such lapses to the author's attention and request that the missing item be supplied.

AQ The footnote, signalled by an asterisk, to Table 4 has no matching callout in the body of the table. Please insert the corresponding asterisk in the table or delete the footnote along with the symbol.

AQ The asterisk in column 4 (or row 2 or whatever) of Table 2 has no corresponding footnote. Please provide the footnote or delete the asterisk.

Missing citations of tables and figures

Every table or figure needs to be cited in the text by its number. If such a citation is missing, the copyeditor should first try to find the corresponding text and insert a formal citation of the table or the figure accompanied by its number, revising the text as appropriate, and seek the author's approval. If this is not possible – the copyeditor may not be familiar enough with the subject matter – the author should be requested to insert appropriate text that mentions the table or the figure by its number.

> **AQ** The citation for Table 1 was not provided in the text. The text has been revised to incorporate the citation. Please confirm whether the revision is acceptable; if it is not, please modify the text and mention the table by its number.

Mismatch between figure caption, figure citation, and artwork

At times, although each figure is mentioned in the text, some elements may be missing within a figure, or the caption may not be adequate. These shortcomings should be brought to the attention of the author.

> **AQ** The caption to Figure 4 mentions a cross symbol, but Figure 4 does not show such a symbol. Please check.

> **AQ** The caption to Figure 4 mentions parts 4A and 4B, but the figure does not show such labels. Please check.

Missing references or elements within references

Academic writing typically features citations (embedded within the text as pointers to the sources of information given in the text) and matching references (listed at the end under the heading 'References' or 'Works cited'), giving full bibliographic details of each source. Each such citation, which may be simply a number (often referred to as the Vancouver system) or comprise the name(s) of the author(s) and the year of publication (the Harvard system). Each citation should have a matching reference, and vice versa, and each reference should give full bibliographic details of the source. Such details vary with the kind of source; for example, if the source is a paper published in a journal, the details include the volume number of the journal and the page range (the first and the last page for the paper being cited). If supplying such missing elements is the copyeditor's responsibility, the copyeditor should try to find the missing bibliographic details from the internet by consulting the appropriate databases or services such as PubMed and Google Scholar, archived issues of the journal, and library catalogues such as WorldCat. If the missing information cannot be found, the author should be requested to supply it (because the author is expected to have had access to each cited source).

Here are some sample queries related to references.

> **AQ** Please provide the initials of the authors or editors in Reference [13].

> **AQ** Please provide the name of the journal (or volume number or page range) in Reference [2].

At times, authors cite their forthcoming articles as 'in press' or 'forthcoming' and are therefore unable to supply full bibliographic information at the time of writing. It is worth querying the author whether the missing details have since become available. It should be noted that such citations are to papers accepted by the journal or publisher but yet to be published: citations to documents 'submitted for publication' or 'in preparation' are seldom acceptable and may be replaced with the phrase 'unpublished data' (no corresponding reference is expected for such citations).

> **AQ** Please update reference 'X et al. (in press)' with year, volume number, and page range if these details are available.

References, figures, tables, equations, boxes, etc. not appearing in order

At times, items are out of sequence and therefore require an appropriate query.

> **AQ** Figure citations were not provided in sequence and have been renumbered as follows; please check whether the revised numbering is correct:
> - Figure 1 is now Figure 3;
> - Figure 2 is now Figure 1;
> - Figure 3 is now Figure 2.

> **AQ** Table 5 was mentioned before Table 4; therefore, Tables 4 and 5 have been interchanged to maintain the correct sequence. Please check whether the rearrangement is now in order.

> **AQ** Several references were out of sequence, but have since been renumbered in the text as well as in the list of references. Please check whether the references are now in order.

Websites

Because the web content is not always permanent, unlike printed sources, most publishers require that references to web pages also include the date on which they were accessed by the author. If such dates are not supplied, request the author to insert the most recent date on which the author had accessed the web page in question.

> **AQ** Please give the latest date on which you accessed the webpage.

Similarly, every link should be current and working. If the copyeditor is unable to access the web page in question using the link supplied by the author, the fact should be brought to the author's attention.

> **AQ** The provided web site link dose not work. Please provide the correct link.

Units of measurement

If the style specifies that values of the variables be expressed using the International System of Units (usually referred to as SI units, short for French Système International d'Unités), request the author to provide the values in appropriate SI units.

> **AQ** As the journal follows the SI units, please convert the distances given in miles into kilometres.

Missing addresses of suppliers or manufacturers of chemicals and equipment

Typically, in the Methods section of a research paper, the authors are expected to supply the make, the model, the manufacturer, and the manufacturer's location for any scientific instruments, devices, or chemicals used in the research being reported in the manuscript. If such details are missing, see if you can supply them yourself and ask the author to confirm them; if not, request the author to supply the relevant details.

> **AQ** Please provide the name, city, state, and country for the manufacturer of the instrument or device (and its make and model) or for the manufacturer of the chemicals used when these are first mentioned.

To conclude, author queries should be polite, clear, and concise. Only well-written queries help editors to get the required information from authors and thereby give readers a better product.

Divya Jyoti Munjal (djmunjal@gmail.com) is a publishing professional with more than 19 years of experience in the industry. Her expertise is in the field of client servicing, project management, problem solving, and copyediting books and journals. In her free time, she reads spiritual and self-help books and records spiritual podcasts. She has a BSc (Hons) degree in zoology, a master's degree in history, and another master's degree in education.

CHAPTER 13

Basics of Fact-Checking for Editors

Sayantani De

If the character of author Lalmohan Ganguly in the Bengali film *Sonar Kella* is to be believed, a camel can walk for days without having a drop of water even in a desert, because it can store water in its stomach. Ganguly, who writes under the pseudonym Jatayu, was lucky to have the sleuth Feluda, an easy-going listener, who corrected him and asked that right information be printed in the seventh edition of his crime fiction *Sahara-ey Siharan*, but a discerning reader may well raise concern over the quality of writing and the merit of the author. In turn, both can impact the reputation of the publisher. Fact-checking, a critical but often overlooked element in the publishing process, can help in publishing books, research papers, blogs, news – all forms of communication materials that need to be vetted for factual correctness.

According to the *Cambridge Learners Dictionary*, the term 'fact-checking' refers to "the process of checking that all the facts in a piece of writing . . . are correct" (https://tinyurl.com/dictengfact). Fact-checking is important not only for validating the correctness of the information used by the author in the present context, but also for providing definitive and historically accurate perspectives. Fact-checking also helps to establish authors, their research and writing, and the act of publishing their work – either by a media house or by a publishing house – as an ethical enterprise in keeping with the tenets of scholarly publishing. Although many may believe that only non-fiction and academic titles need fact-checking, works of fiction are on a more slippery ground: the demands of the narrative and an urge to justify the trajectory of characters may make the author overlook historical accuracy of dates, events, and other facts. Although traditionally newsrooms have been the cradle of fact-checking, in the era of post-truth and the rise of social media, with sensational, and often unverified, facts attracting more eyeballs, fact-checking is more important than ever, irrespective of the nature of the communication material.

SIGNIFICANCE OF FACT-CHECKING IN THE POST-TRUTH ERA

'Post-truth', adjudged the 'Oxford Dictionaries Word of the Year 2016' (https://languages.oup.com/word-of-the-year/2016/), is an adjective, defined as "relating to or denoting circumstances in which objective facts are less influential in shaping public opinion than appeals to emotion and personal belief." In the past decade, the use of 'alternative facts' to build narratives that sway the popular opinion has increased significantly, driven by social-media platforms. Pandering to innate human biases, the trend is driving social and political changes across the world and was termed as a 'dangerous nihilistic idea' by Indian-American columnist and political commentator Fareed Zakaria (https://transcripts.cnn.com/show/fzgps/date/2018-04-15/segment/01). Explaining the importance of the word and the concept, the 'Oxford Languages' website (https://languages.oup.com/word-of-the-year/2016/) observes: "Post-truth has gone from being a peripheral term to being a mainstay in political commentary, now often being used by major publications without the need for clarification or definition in their headlines."

Although there is no doubt that the internet has democratized access to information, constant technical advancement in the form of artificial intelligence and algorithms, close to human intelligence but incapable of judging nuances and yet deciding what we see and read, has made fact-checking mandatory and tricky. As governments across the world increasingly turn totalitarian and show protectionist tendencies, access to objective facts has become a more necessary but more laborious process. Post-truth communiqués are often marked by extreme emotions tending towards inflammatory, biased towards the issuing group, comprising very little facts or twisted facts (indicating lack of objectivity) or even a lie, and have a tendency to present myths and legends as facts. The Taj Mahal, in Agra, Uttar Pradesh, India, one of the seven wonders of the world, is a case in point. According to the historian P N Oak's 1989 book *Taj Mahal: The True Story*, the monument was built in 1155, decades before the Muslim invasion of India, and the name Taj Mahal is a corrupt form of Sanskrit 'Tejo Mahalay', which refers to a Hindu temple on the exact site. A petition to declare that the monument was built by a Hindu ruler was dismissed by the Supreme Court in 2000 (https://tinyurl.com/Fact-check1) and again in 2017, and the Archaeological Survey of India informed the local court that the Taj Mahal is a tomb and not a temple (https://tinyurl.com/Fact-check2).

TYPES OF FACT-CHECKING

Fact-checking can be conducted both before and after a text is published, referred to as ante hoc or post hoc, respectively. If a publisher chooses to employ an in-house fact checker, the process is known as internal fact-checking. However, sometimes, an external or third-party fact checker may be involved, working either solo or as part of the editorial team. Given the vastness of the information universe that calls for fact-checking, being qualified in any one discipline may not be enough to become an efficient fact checker. A generally curious and questioning mind, and an affinity for research, can work better than expertise in any one subject or discipline.

The following are a few key terms that can help a fact checker in improving precision.

Fake news are texts that attract the attention of the reader but are likely to be fabricated, with no verifiable facts, quotes, or sources. Propaganda, employed by administrators since ancient times and mastered by German dictator Adolf Hitler, is a shining example of fake news.

Misinformation refers to unintended spread of false information without harmful intent. Jumping to conclusions without probing into a claim or believing in cures for diseases without looking for scientific data are some examples of misinformation.

Disinformation refers to fabrication and spread of false information with intent to harm someone. Morphed photographs and half-truths that, by concealing information, end up harming the targeted person or community are some examples.

Malinformation refers to the use and spread of genuine information with an intent to expose and harm someone. (See an example later in this chapter under 'Fact-checking using photos, audio clips, and audiovisual material'.)

Alternative facts, a term first used by former US President Donald Trump's White House counsel Kellyanne Conway, refer to any information that is contrary to reality (https://tinyurl.com/Fact-check3) and may include any of the above or even a blatant lie.

HOW TO FACT-CHECK

Fact checkers can use either proprietary information, such as interviews and letters, or information available in the public domain through websites and social media, newspapers and magazines, and books.

Fact checkers working independently with media houses or as a part of their copy desk are more likely to access proprietary information to establish the veracity of a news report. And although publishing houses believe the responsibility of providing correct facts to be that of the author, some may club fact-checking with a copyeditor's other responsibilities.

Most common errors in a text occur in

- names of organizations, places, titles, etc.
- statistics and historical facts
- date, time, season, location, distance, and physical descriptions
- argument or narrative that depends on a particular fact.

In using information available only in the public domain, fact-checking can be done through text, audio clips, audio–video files, and photos. However, text and photos are more easily accessible and hence are more relied on. Here are some guidelines for fact checkers.

Fact-checking using text

- Be mindful of the source of the information. Information from the government and reputable educational institutions can be used as is. However, information available solely with organizations with a declared history of bias should be verified from at least two other credible sources. Irrespective of the source, it is always advisable to read the fine print instead of the whole gamut of information: look for specific data (individual facts, statistics, or items of information) in the set of information (data that are processed, organized, and structured to provide context and enable decision-making) to identify the nuances and exact points where tweaks have been made. Draw the author's attention to any view that is authoritative but contrarian to the government data as it may contribute to fine-tuning the author's argument and will not only add to the accuracy of facts and the quality of copyediting but also help in addressing queries at any stage.

- Never rely solely on any information that is available on platforms such as Wikipedia. Always verify the information from multiple sources. This is because Wikipedia (as part of the non-profit Wikimedia Foundation) was modelled (in 2011, much before the advent of social media) as a platform to write for people not connected with media or research institutions (https://www.britannica.com/topic/Wikipedia). Users with credentials can edit the information that is usually supported by external links. Examining these reference links at top right of the block of text that contains the information and listed at the end of the article can be a good starting point.
- In using the internet to verify information, domain names in the URL can indicate whether they are a reliable source. In India, government-owned websites usually have the extension '.gov.in' and educational institutions have the extension '.ac.in'. Outside India, usually, '.gov' indicates a government-owned website and '.edu' indicates an educational institution.
- In the case of educational institutions, before entering a specific website, it is helpful to check the institution's ranking. In India, one can verify the credentials of an educational institution by consulting the University Grants Commission's (UGC's) list of fake universities and the National Institutional Ranking Framework (NIRF) created by the Ministry of Education.
- Avoid using sources such as press releases, company websites, and personal websites as the sole source of information. Treat such information as a verified fact only after in-depth research. Reputed media houses have started using a feature known as timestamp to prevent misinformation. The *Guardian* applies

bright yellow labels to all news stories that are older than six months (https://tinyurl.com/ethicsandnews).

Fact-checking using photos, audio clips, and audiovisual material

- Carefully observe the entire photograph or video – not merely the object(s) of interest – and compare what you see with the claim being examined. Any mismatch – colour of a leaf, writing on a billboard, attire of people, etc. – can yield useful clues supporting or contesting the claim.
- If a claim is being verified with the help of only audio clips, make efforts to establish that the voice belongs to the intended speaker. You may seek more audio clips or use online resources to obtain more samples of the voice to establish the identity of its owner.
- Use methods such as Google Lens to see if the photograph was published before and if so, check its details.
- Use such fact-checking websites as Alt News in India to check if they have already examined the photo, audio, or video.

SOME EXAMPLES OF FACT-CHECKING

Nepal

In February 2021, social-media users shared a photo of a political rally in Nepal's capital city, Kathmandu, showing an Indian flag amid flags of the splinter faction of the Nepal Communist Party. The photo sparked a controversy and fuelled conspiracy theories that India was involved in the opposition to the-then Prime Minister of Nepal. The South Asia Check, an independent non-profit initiative by Panos South Asia, used a Google reverse-image search and keyword search that traced the photo to a previous rally and established the Indian flag as 'artificially inserted' (https://tinyurl.com/Fact-check5). Deeper research revealed that those who shared the news were close to the ruling party, which aimed to discredit the opposition rally. The original photo was taken by Annapurna Post photographers on 29 December 2020.

India

On 3 November 2021, a Twitter user shared a clip of arson at a petrol pump, claiming the incident took place in Tripura and that the police had taken no action. The clip was also shared widely on WhatsApp, and many requested the fact-checking outlet Alt News to verify the claim.

Within the "opening few seconds of the video", Alt News found "that the incident could be from Pakistan based on the clothes worn by the people and the dialect they can be heard speaking." Alt News staff performed multiple keyword searches using 'Pakistan petrol pump explosion' on YouTube, which led them to a news report by the Pakistan-based Samaa TV dated 29 October 2021 (https://tinyurl.com/Fact-check6).

As a rule of thumb, look for platforms that are compliant with the principles of the International Fact-Checking Network (IFCN), a unit of the Poynter Institute. The list of verified signatories from India, as in February 2022, include the following[1]:

- FactChecker.in
- FactCrescendo
- First Check
- NewsMobile
- Newschecker
- Newsmeter
- Soft Media Hub LLP
- THIP Healthtech Pvt Ltd

1 https://ifcncodeofprinciples.poynter.org/signatories (since 29 April 2020, AltNews is no longer a signatory to the IFCN. Ref: Co-founder's Tweet available at https://twitter.com/zoo_bear/status/1360595355759304713?lang=en).

- TV Today Network Limited (India Today)
- The Logical Indian
- VishvasNews (MMI Online Limited)
- Youturn
- Factly Media & Research
- The Quint.

SHOULD EDITORS CHECK FACTS?

The answer is both yes and no, depending on the precise nature of the editing job. It is true that one cannot be a master of all, but fact-checking allows one to be 'correct' without depending on memory. For example, during the pandemic, the World Health Organization (WHO) has been in the news far more than other times. In keeping with the trend, we may expect many works of fiction to be set during the period of the coronavirus pandemic and mention the WHO. A copyeditor, especially someone handling medical and scientific text, is likely to come across the fully spelt-out form of WHO more frequently than in normal times. However, it is quite possible that someone dealing with text in British English, especially in news media, would choose to use 'organisation' (with an 's'), which is incorrect in this case because 'World Health Organization' is a proper noun, and spelt thus, irrespective of the variety of English that the rest of the text follows. Similarly, copyeditors dealing with corporate and business texts using US English should be mindful in spelling out OECD: The official version – Organisation for Economic Co-operation and Development – uses 's', and the spelling has to be retained, even if the word sports a red underline in a Microsoft Word file or Google docs. Similarly, copyeditors must check for correct hyphenation and prepositions, because the possibility of using cooperation instead of the official form co-operation or 'of' instead of 'for' cannot be ruled out.

Although some publishing houses ask copyeditors to fact-check texts, independent professionals may resent the step. However, even seemingly obvious matters such as spelling, numbers, or grammar may require copyeditors to verify the text and refer to the source for the right one. In doing so, the copyeditor acts as a fact checker for making the text as free of errors as possible. As a rule of thumb, copyeditors must go to the source to verify anything that is new to them or raises suspicions, for example, use of such superlatives as only, first, and most. For information that requires verification, it is advisable to query the author but accept only legitimate sources. Besides, anyone undertaking developmental editing, a job that identifies gaps in plots and narratives, among other things, may find fact-checking a useful value-added service, especially if working as an independent consultant. With self-publishing and indie publishing houses gathering steam, more mindful of nuances of ethics and competing with the traditional publishing houses, one can hope that fact-checking gets its fair share in both fiction and non-fiction.

EDUCATIONAL RESOURCES TO IMPROVE FACT-CHECKING SKILLS

Most of the professional fact checkers in India and many other parts of the world ply their trade on the basis of their vast professional experience as journalists, editors in publishing houses, or scholars. Fact-checking as a specialization is rarely encountered in India, but those who are interested in pursuing this line of work can complete certificate courses from Poynter Institute and NYU School of Professional Studies, or functional training offered by Google News Initiative, AFP Fact Check, and the Reuters training course on digital journalism, to mention a few. All these courses are offered online: the functional training offered by Google News Initiative, AFP Fact Check, and the Reuters course is available for free, whereas Poynter Institute offers both free and paid versions, depending on the level and the type of course. Being a fact checker may not open a wide choice of job opportunities in India at present, but the scenario is changing as leading digital portals increasingly double as fact-checking platforms to retain credibility and attract a wider audience. Having a certificate can be useful in seizing the opportunities such development may open in the future.

CONCLUSION

In the Western world, fact-checking is now an established part of publishing. Owing to the changing sociocultural conditions, India too is catching up fast, so much so that the Government of India has also launched a platform to verify central-government-related news: the PIB Fact Check is run by the Press Information Bureau to counter misinformation on government policies and schemes. Although Indian news and media houses have addressed the information gap better by establishing and popularizing fact-checking as an essential component of publishing, it is imperative and possibly urgent for Indian publishing houses to introduce this extra step as a policy, for both their and their authors' long-term reputation, because we are responsible for developing and expanding the intellectual capabilities of both ourselves and the generations to come.

Sayantani De (connectwithsayantani@gmail.com) is a former journalist and a communication professional with 15 years of experience in mainstream and B2B media, public relations, and management consultancy. She gained her experience in reporting and editing news on science and technology, renewable energy, health care, politics, and foreign affairs during her tenure with the Press Trust of India, Energy Next, *The Statesman*, and corporate majors Aptara and WNS. She holds master's degrees in English literature and mass communication and enjoys working outside her comfort zone. In 2021, she co-founded RudderFit Consulting, a multidisciplinary, purpose-driven content and communication solutions advisory firm that helps businesses to steer their way through changing communications trends.

PART IV

Allied Services

CHAPTER 14

An Introduction to Proofreading

Denise Cowle

PROOFREADING IN THE PUBLISHING WORKFLOW

It is important to understand where proofreading lies in the traditional publishing process, as that has a direct impact on what you, as the proofreader, should and should not be doing at this stage. We also need to consider how this process may differ when proofreading for self-publishers and organizations that are not publishers but, nevertheless, create and publish written materials. Let us take a look at what convention dictates as the traditional workflow and where proofreading fits into it.

In Figure 14.1 we can see that proofreading is the final stage in the publishing workflow before the book or journal article is printed. The work is done on a PDF file that the typesetter produces, which shows the book or article as it will appear when printed.

The difference between proofreading and copyediting

Figure 14.1 also indicates where the roles of the copyeditor and the proofreader differ. The copyeditor typically works in Microsoft Word or some other word-processing software package and prepares the file for typesetting, ensuring that the content is presented consistently, is free of spelling and grammatical errors, and follows house style.

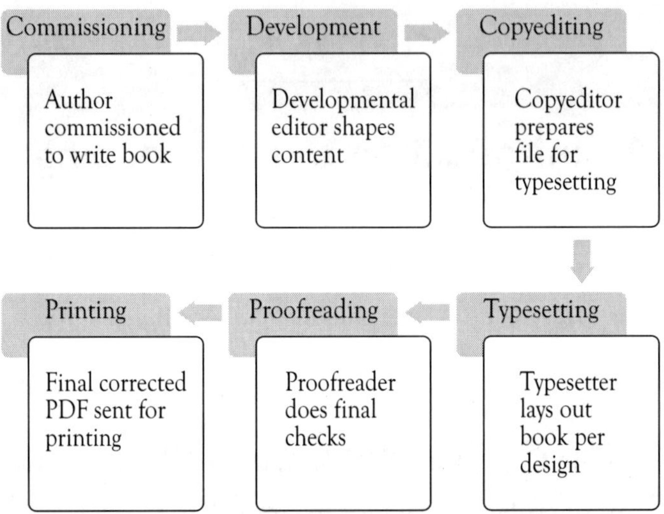

Figure 14.1 Traditional publishing workflow.

The proofreader works on a PDF file produced by the typesetter to make final checks to identify any remaining errors missed during copyediting and those introduced at the design stage. The proofreader also checks the layout and formatting of the designed file.

So we can see that substantial changes to content should happen early in the process, working in Word or any other word-processing package (as distinct from a page layout package such as InDesign). Once the manuscript has been typeset, the proofreader focuses on outright errors and formatting issues and marks up the PDF file for the typesetter to make the corrections in the source file (that is, the file used for generating the PDF file).

It is usual to have several rounds of proofreading, with the PDF file going back and forth between the proofreader and the designer to make sure all the corrections have been taken into the file correctly.

The purpose of proofreading: who do we proofread for?

When we proofread, we must be mindful of the expectations of those who are invested in us doing a thorough job at this stage.

Publishers. Primarily, the proofreader is employed by publishers to ensure that their product is as free from errors as possible. You could also consider this a quality-assurance check.

Authors. As the proofreader, you have a responsibility to the authors to ensure that their work is presented clearly and accurately. You are protecting their reputation.

Typesetters. Your role here is to communicate essential changes to the typesetter to implement them in the source file. It is essential that your markup is clear and unambiguous if the typesetter is to understand your intentions and work efficiently.

Readers. Errors and omissions distract readers from the content of a book or article and may even cause them to abandon it. You are serving the readers by making sure their reading experience is a pleasant one, as free from distractions as possible.

What a proofreader should do

As a proofreader, you do not make changes directly to the file, which is why we refer to marking up: you mark up the PDF file, indicating what corrections are needed, and the typesetter implements those changes in the design software (the source file).

First proofs

At first proofs, the proofreader checks that the content has been imported into the typesetting software correctly: that all the text is there, it is correct, and it is styled, laid out, and cross-referenced properly. The publisher's brief should tell you specifically what is to be checked at this stage. In complex layouts, such as educational materials, it is not unusual for some elements to not yet be finalized, for example artwork or photo permissions. You might refer to this as production proofreading.

Second proofs

At second proofs, the proofreader makes sure all corrections marked on the first proofs have been correctly implemented and no new errors introduced. Artwork that was supplied after the first proofs were proofread is also checked. You may know this stage as editorial proofreading. In the Western world, production proofreading is not considered distinct from editorial proofreading, and the term proofreading covers all of the tasks required at both stages.

Third proofs and beyond

Third proofs are usually the point at which a final file is signed off as being ready for printing. However, depending on the process leading up to proofreading, and how much work had to be done at first and second proofs, further rounds may be required. The process may go on to fourth or even fifth proofs. (And I've worked on seventh and eighth proofs before!) The law of diminishing returns tells us that there will be a point at which the time and money spent on further rounds are no longer effective, and we have to accept that the file is 'good enough'. This is a concept that we must be comfortable with if we are to avoid continually tweaking the text without making any substantive improvements to it.

What a proofreader should not do

We can see that at the proofreading stage we are not editing the content. It is a quality-assurance process to ensure that the copyedited manuscript has been correctly imported to the design software – for example, sometimes formatting such as bold and italic can be lost or corrupted in the process – and that the text is laid out correctly.

Marking up the PDF file

The proofreader's markup may be applied using one or more of the following methods:

- highlighting and sticky notes
- text boxes and call-out boxes
- Adobe inbuilt commenting tools
- imported stamps[1]

The focus is on ensuring that publishing conventions and client preferences have been adhered to, for example

- house style for formatting and layout
- hierarchy of headings
- labelling and cross-referencing of figures, tables, and images
- page numbers, correct headers and footers that match the table of contents.

You will also be expected to catch any errors of commission or omission, that is those that have been missed during editing or introduced during typesetting.

When proofreading, you should be given the overarching house style guide and the copyeditor's style sheet for this specific project to refer to, so you are not second-guessing decisions that have already been made.

Proofreading for non-publishers and self-publishers

For organizations that are not publishers but produce lots of content, and for self-publishers managing their own writing and publishing process, the process is much more fluid. Here, the definitions of different levels of editing and proofreading may be blurred, and we cannot assume that non-publishers and self-publishers will use the terms copyediting and proofreading in the same way.

1 https://tinyurl.com/proofstamp

Your client may ask for proofreading but actually mean – and need – a heavy copyedit. Or you may be presented with a fully designed report or book in PDF that has not been through any form of editing beforehand. Understanding what the client wants and whether this can be achieved at the proofreading stage involves careful communication and a clear articulation of expectations on both sides.

For example, it is always preferable to edit in a Word file or equivalent, as long as the editing is carried out before typesetting or before page make-up, but if the document is already designed and laid out in a PDF your client must understand the limitations this will impose. You will be marking up changes for the designer to implement, which could have a significant cost implication, not to mention the knock-on effects on the layout. A six-page marketing flyer may only need a few comments, which could easily be managed by the designer. But if the writing needs much heavier intervention, then marking up on a PDF file becomes unwieldy and there is a significant risk of introducing errors when large amounts of text need to be moved, cut, or added at this stage.

Proof-editing

The budgetary restrictions of many self-publishers and small businesses may preclude multiple rounds of editing and proofreading in the traditional sense. So for these clients it may be that a proof-edit of their document in Word or equivalent before it is typeset is the best option.

Proof-editing is a single pass through the document to address as many issues as possible that would usually be dealt with in separate copyediting and proofreading passes. The client may decide that this is where their money is best spent and where you, the proofreader, can be most effective. You both have to trust that any mistakes still present at the design stage will be minor.

THE PROOFREADER'S SKILLS

Many of us come to proofreading because we have an eye for spotting typos and grammatical errors, but there is much more to it than that! Having a good knowledge of English spelling, punctuation, and grammar is an excellent starting point, but professional proofreaders require other, equally important, skills if they are to do their job effectively.

Reading with intent

The average person will read a text at about 200–250 words per minute, or 12,000–15,000 words per hour. A professional proofreader may work at a rate of 2,500 words per hour, which is about a fifth of that speed. Why is that?

When we read for pleasure, or to extract information, our brain processes the text in chunks, and we anticipate what is coming without slowing down to absorb every individual word and character. This is an effective way of reading to take in content, but not an effective way of analysing it for errors. This is why we are not very good at proofreading our own writing – our brain is so familiar with the content that it skips over any errors.

To proofread effectively we need to slow down and really examine what is on the page. Instead of processing the text in chunks, we need to digest each word individually to ensure it is actually there and correctly spelt.

Spelling, punctuation, and grammar

An excellent grasp of spelling, punctuation, and grammar is essential for a professional proofreader. However, being good at English at school, or even being in possession of a university degree, is not necessarily enough. The rules we learnt at school may have changed since, or they may not even have been rules in the first place but merely style choices.

We have to approach language use with an open mind and be willing to unlearn these 'rules', know when it is OK to break them, and be able to explain them to our clients, who may challenge our corrections.

More than ever, publishing is a global industry, and you may find yourself working with clients who use different Englishes. Being aware of the variations of conventions between, for example, British English, US English, Australian English, and Canadian English, to name a few, avoids the situation where you incorrectly impose what you believe to be 'correct' usage.

An eye for detail

Proofreading goes beyond the text that is on the page. The proofreader is often the first person to see the book in its entirety, and identifying inconsistencies in formatting and layout is an integral part of the job. For example, consider the following questions.

- Can you spot inconsistent page depths, or that the page numbers in the table of contents do not match the page numbers in the body of the work?
- Do you understand the correct use of hyphens, en dashes, and em dashes and can you identify and correct where the design software has converted all dashes to hyphens in error?
- Can you spot a full stop that is bold where it should not be?
- Would you spot that an image has been flipped so that the caption is now incorrect?

Identifying and dealing with these details is important for presenting a professional, polished final product. Professional editorial training will help you to take a systematic approach that ensures you know what to look for and how to manage it.

Working to a brief

Publishers should provide a proofreader with a brief that outlines exactly what they want checked, and this will vary depending on the project and which stage of proofreading the work is at.

Without a brief you risk spending your time (and their budget) on unnecessary work, potentially undoing decisions that have been made earlier in the editing process. If you are not sent a brief, ask for it, and for the house style guide and copyeditor's style sheet. This ensures that you know exactly what is required of you, as the scope of your work will be clearly defined.

Being organized and methodical

As proofreaders, our approach must be organized and methodical if we are to maximize our effectiveness. A piecemeal or scattergun approach to our work can only result in poor performance: inefficient at best, ineffective at worst. Being organized starts with how we approach our work.

- Do I have everything I need for this project?
- Have I organized my schedule properly to make enough space for it?
- Am I clear on the deliverables and the deadline?
- Is my workstation set up to maximize my efficiency?
- Do I have any reference works I might need to hand?
- Do I have enough screen real estate to display the project optimally?

How we choose to approach our work may vary from one project to the next, and from one proofreader to another. But one thing all professional proofreaders share is a structured approach to their work. This may involve the use of checklists, from a general list that applies to every job to the specific, based on details in the brief. For efficiency, multiple passes through the text may be required, each concentrating on different points.

However you choose to organize your work, bringing structure and order to your approach will make you both more efficient and more effective.

Staying within the scope

Once you have read the brief and understood what is involved in the project, stick to it! Tempting as it may be to mark changes to make sentences read better, or because you have found a better way of expressing something, this is not your job. That sentence may be the result of extensive discussions between the editor and author, and they will not want it changed. Beware of imposing your personal preferences for word choice and style on your clients. If there is something that you feel strongly should be changed, flag it in a note to the editor when you return the file.

WHAT THE PROOFREADER LOOKS FOR

So the project is on our desk: what will we actually be expected to do in a typical proofread?

Following a brief and applying the house style

From the brief we should extract the key issues the client wants us to address. You can use these points to create a project checklist.

Literal and typographical errors

Errors can be missed during copyediting, but they can also be introduced during the typesetting process.

Style and formatting errors

There are many small ways in which the appearance of the text on the page can go wrong. For example

- bold and italic inconsistently applied or missing

- capitals, including small capitals, inconsistently applied
- inconsistent hyphenation
- diacritics in names not retained through the typesetting process.

Layout and design errors

Taking an overview of how the text sits on the page will include checking for

- consistent page depth and margins
- running headers and footers matching the table of contents and positioned correctly
- correct spacing above and below headings
- bad word breaks at the end of lines
- extra spaces introduced between or within words
- bullet lists positioned and punctuated correctly.

Labelling of figures, tables, and images

When the text includes figures or tables, it is essential that you take the time to carefully check they are presented correctly. Your checklist should include

- all figures and tables numbered consecutively
- all in-text references to these elements correct
- all captions accurate and reflect content.

Table of contents and internal cross-references to pages

You may be asked to populate the table of contents with the correct page numbers and insert them for all internal cross-references. If they are already in place, you will be expected to check them carefully, so that the reader is directed to the correct pages.

References and bibliography

Check that references are numbered correctly in the text, each has a corresponding entry in the reference list, and the list of references is styled correctly. If any of the references are incomplete or missing, flag them for attention.

The same applies to the bibliography. It should be presented according to house style: you will identify any errors or deviation from the style and mark them up appropriately.

SUMMARY

Proofreading is one of the final stages in the publishing workflow and is the last opportunity for errors to be identified and corrections implemented. It requires an excellent understanding of language, an organized and methodical approach, and a keen eye for detail. The value of a good proofreader should not be underestimated!

COURSES

The following organizations provide training in editing and proofreading. Some are delivered in live online classes, whereas others are asynchronous webinars you can access at a time that suits you.

United Kingdom

The Chartered Institute of Editing and Proofreading (https://www.ciep.uk/)
The Publishing Training Centre (https://www.publishingtrainingcentre.co.uk/)

United States

ACES: The Society for Editing (https://aceseditors.org/)
The Editorial Freelancers Association (https://www.the-efa.org/)

Australia

The Institute of Professional Editors (https://www.iped-editors.org/)

The author of this chapter also provides a self-paced video course on marking up PDF page proofs: 'How to mark up PDF page proofs' (https://bit.ly/PDFmarkup). Members of the Indian Copyeditors Forum are eligible for a 20% discount code for the course.

Denise Cowle (denise@denisecowleeditorial.com) is an editor of non-fiction specializing in education and business materials. Based in Scotland, she is an Advanced Professional Member of the Chartered Institute of Editing and Proofreading (CIEP) and has served on its Council first as Marketing Director and now as Vice-Chair, since 2017. She is a tutor for Publishing Scotland and the CIEP.

CHAPTER 15

Alt Text Writing

Opportunities to Learn and Earn

Visalakshy Loganathan

Publishing an article or a book involves many professionals with different skills mostly working in sequence and sometimes in tandem.

'Alt text' – short for 'alternative text' – writing is one such task in publishing and involves supplying text as an alternative to images so that visually impaired readers who cannot see the images can make some sense of them, typically by listening to the alternative text with the help of a screen reader. The images may be part of a book, presentations using PowerPoint or similar software packages, interactive elements on a web page, animations, and even entire videos.

To work as an alt text writer, one should possess good writing and analytical skills and expertise in a particular area such as medicine, chemistry, maths, physics, or engineering. Professionals who are already in publishing, such as project managers, copyeditors, and indexers, may find it easier to acquire this additional skill, which could open up new growth opportunities for them.

Although alt text writing is a highly skilled job, one could acquire the skills within a short time by undergoing formal training and then work either as freelance or as an in-house alt text writer.

Alt text writers are in great demand in India and abroad, which is why this is the right time to learn the craft and start on a lucrative career in alt text writing.

HISTORY OF ALT TEXT

Let us begin by looking at how alt text writing came into existence and its history and then study some examples of alt text from popular media.

Alt text was developed to comply with the provisions of various accessibility acts passed in the United States – legislation that aimed at making books, websites, etc. accessible even to those who are visually challenged and thus changed the way people used information.

Rehabilitation Act of 1973

The first such act was the Rehabilitation Act of 1973. People with severe disabilities were discriminated against and were excluded from being considered for various jobs. To redress this inequity, the act provided for vocational rehabilitation of people with disabilities. They were given free training to be independent and be able to secure a job, thus paving the way towards reducing the discrimination against them in the job market.

Before we come to the next piece of legislation, let us be a bit clear about what disability means. Disability is an umbrella term for a whole gamut of impairments that include visual impairment, hearing impairment, physical impairment, etc. The category includes not only those born with disabilities or burdened with them at a young age but also older people who lose their faculties because of old age and those with less severe disabilities such as dyslexia, partial blindness, and deafness.

Section 508 (1986)

Section 508, which was passed in 1986, is an addition to the Rehabilitation Act of 1973 and provided access to information in electronic form including that on websites. For example, people may receive telephone calls giving them important information on upcoming elections or taxes. The information may also be disseminated through local newspapers or other channels or given out through pamphlets. Section 508 ensured that older people and people with less severe disabilities were also able to receive such information with ease. By extension, this law applies to present-day websites too. In the United States, it is mandatory for a website to be compliant with Section 508. A comprehensive checklist that covers such compliance is available at https://tinyurl.com/2eat4wbh.

Americans with Disabilities Act of 1990

The law that proved to be the turning point in the history of the United States, especially in the field of education, was the Americans with Disabilities Act, which was passed in 1990. The act helped in improving the lives and inclusivity of people with disabilities. Some of the changes that were made as a consequence of the act include

- separate parking spaces
- wheelchair accessibility in buildings, public transport, and public spaces
- improvements in telecommunication services, such as text-to-speech software and larger fonts on websites
- access to educational materials in the form of electronic media, thereby introducing alt text, closed captioning, etc. (Closed captions refer to displaying spoken words or other sounds as text to make the lessons accessible to the hearing impaired but are also useful to viewers who struggle to understand speakers with different accents.)

21st Century Communications and Video Accessibility Act, 2010

The latest in the series of acts is the 21st Century Communications and Video Accessibility Act of 2010, which provided access to advanced telecommunication products and streaming services such as live streaming of sports or awards shows with closed captioning and audio descriptions of TV shows in Netflix, Hulu, Amazon Prime, etc.

Accessibility guidelines in India

On 3 December 2015, the Department of Empowerment of Persons with Disabilities launched the 'Accessible India campaign' (*Sugamya Bharat Abhiyan*) as a nationwide campaign to achieve universal accessibility for persons with disabilities. The campaign has three major verticals, namely the built environment, transport, and the ecosystem comprising information and communication technologies, of which the last is relevant to this chapter.

Accessibility in the information and communication technologies ecosystem

Access to information takes many forms such as the ability to read price tags, negotiating entry points into museums and exhibitions, decoding a railway timetable, and understanding printed text that gives information essential for health and well-being. As the Accessible India campaign asserts, "No longer should societal barriers of infrastructure, and inaccessible formats stand in the way of obtaining and utilizing information in daily life" (https://tinyurl.com/alt-txt).

ACCESSIBLE PUBLISHING

E-books

In traditional publishing, books are published in print form; in modern publishing, e-books not only capture in digital form all that the print version has but supplement it with add-ons such as online learning materials for students, teaching materials for instructors, activities, and quizzes – and all the images, the visual elements in such e-books, require alt text if the images are to be of any use to the visually impaired.

Presentations

Presentations, which make use of PowerPoint or other similar software packages, are often used by teachers to supplement their lectures, and any images that are part of such presentations require alt text to help the visually impaired students.

Web-based learning

Websites and applications such as Khan Academy, edx, Coursera, BYJU'S, and Vedanta are popular web-learning platforms. They provide closed captioning and also audio descriptions to explain the contents of equations and diagrams.

DEFINITION AND USES OF ALT TEXT

Definition of alt text

Alt text is a textual description of any visual content such as photos, charts, infographics, and illustrations. Alt text "adds context and describes in words information that sighted readers will get by looking at the image" (https://tinyurl.com/acesusa).

Technical definition of alt text

"Alt text is an HTML attribute: alt. When including an image in digital content, an editing or publishing tool tags the image with an HTML tag: <img> . . . Any content that uses HTML tags can include alt text, and many platforms build in the opportunity to add it" (https://aceseditors.org/news/2020/how-to-write-great-alt-text-and-why-it-matters).

WHERE IS ALT TEXT USED

As we have seen earlier, alt text is used as a substitute for images and other graphics in e-books, in web-learning applications, and for images in social media and commercial websites.

But why do we need alt text? One of the main reasons is to make the content of images accessible to the visually impaired. Alt text is also useful for search engine optimization. For example, if your website consists only of photos, you would need some help in bringing traffic to your website, because web crawlers may not be able to index purely visual content. Providing alt-text – which remains hidden from normal viewers – for the photos helps search engines to pick up the words and index the content of your website.

Alt text is also useful when bandwidth is limited or internet connection is slow or when forms other than text are not supported by a device. The text then substitutes for those forms to make their content accessible to the website visitor handicapped by the shortcomings of the device or of the signal.

For example, Netflix provides audio descriptions for some of its more popular series and videos.

Alt text is not the only aspect of accessible publishing but is just a part of it.

TEXT-TO-SPEECH SOFTWARE

Text-to-speech software is required to access alt text for images and other content that require such text. Here are some of the software packages used by publishing companies and individuals.

IBM Watson and Amazon Polly have earned good reviews because they have voices that sound natural. Both allow you to change the gender, the voice, and the accent of speakers to suit your preference.

JAWS is a more commonly used package but deploys a robotic voice.

NaturalReader and Capti Voice are two more packages; the latter is collaborating with schools to provide accessible education to children.

GUIDELINES FOR WRITING GOOD AND USEFUL ALT TEXT

Images can be classified as decorative or non-decorative. Decorative images are present only for aesthetic purposes, whereas non-decorative images convey useful information in addition to the caption. Hence, it is not necessary to add alt text for decorative images. Let us see a few examples of decorative images. In Figure 15.1, the image on the left is a logo element used in the title of a document; the image on the right can also be considered decorative because it presents no useful or essential information. A good rule of thumb is to check whether any information will be lost if the image is removed.

Figure 15.1 Two purely decorative images: left, a logotype (SOURCE https://www.pinterest.com/); right, an image with little informative content (SOURCE https://www.istockphoto.com/).

Some images such as photos require only a short description of about 15–20 words or fewer than 250 characters. Other images such as graphs, flowcharts, and technical diagrams require more explanation and hence longer descriptions are required. The image in Figure 15.2 requires only a short alt text, such as 'A man holding a clipboard and looking up at the stocked shelves in a warehouse', whereas the image in Figure 15.3 cannot be explained within 250 characters, usually the limit for alt text for any given image, and requires a longer text if it is to convey any useful and reasonably complete information to the listener. The short alt text could be 'A histogram shows the frequency of comorbidities in different age groups' and the longer text could be 'A histogram shows the frequency of comorbidities in different age groups: the X axis shows age groups from 20 to 100 in increments of 10. The Y axis shows the frequency of comorbidities from 0 to 5.0 in increments of 1.0. The age groups and the corresponding frequencies for comorbidities are as follows: 20 to 30, 2.0; 30 to 40, 4.0; 40 to 50, 4.0; 50 to 60, 5.0; 60 to 70, 3.0; 70 to 80, 1.0; 90 to 100, 1.0'.

Figure 15.2 An image that requires only short alt text (SOURCE https://www.freepik.com/).

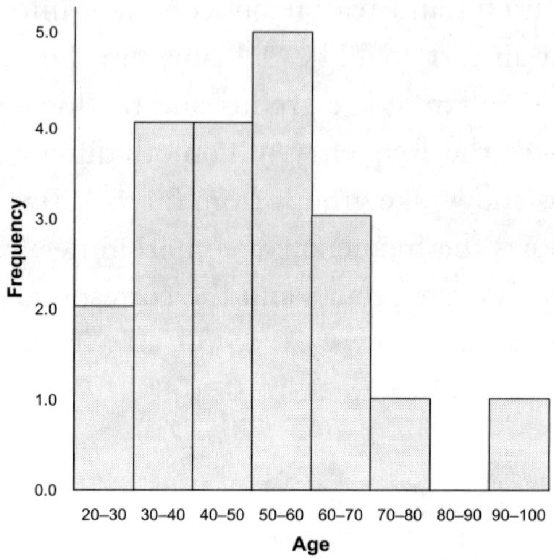

Figure 15.3 An image that requires both short and long alt texts.

Alt text should not merely repeat the caption. For Figure 15.4, alt text such as 'An illustration shows genes on chromosome X' would add little value and hence should be avoided. A more appropriate version would be 'An illustration shows chromosome X divided into multiple segments, each corresponding to one gene'.

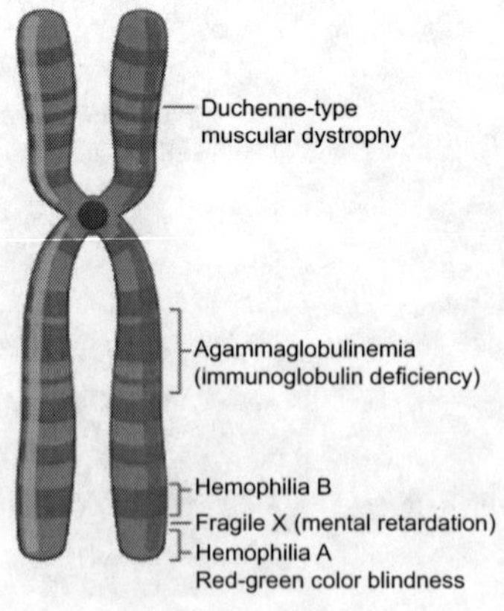

Figure 15.4 Genes on chromosome X (SOURCE https://www.slideshare.net/).

An image must be described based on the context, that is only the information pertinent to the context must be included. The same photo can convey different information in different contexts. For example, if a photo shows a bowl of fruits, the alt text for the photo for a book on nutrition would be different from that for a book on arts. Figure 15.5 is an example of an image for which the context is critical.

For Figure 15.5, a description that reads 'A cartoon shows a pig walking' would be too general, with no indication of the context in which the image appears. A more appropriate alt text would be 'A cartoon shows Peppa walking'. Giving the cartoon character's name, Peppa, personalizes the connection with the listener.

Figure 15.5 An image that needs context (SOURCE https://www.pinterest.com/).

Alt text should not include assumptions or interpretations of the image (Figure 15.6). Alt text that reads 'A photo shows a person washing their hands to remove harmful bacteria and germs' is an interpretation of the image, and such descriptions should be avoided. A more appropriate version would be 'A pair of hands being washed with soap under a running tap'.

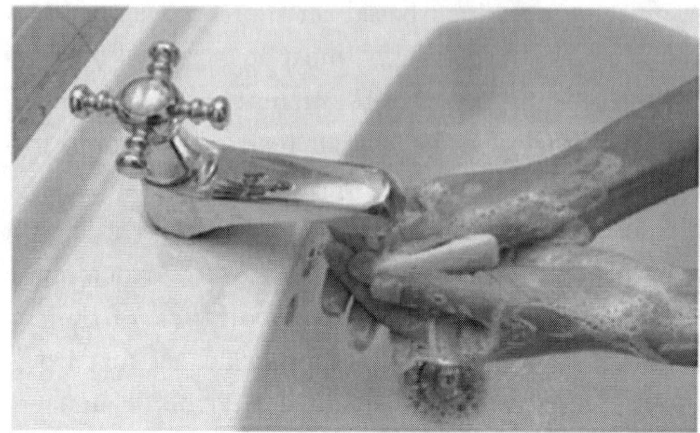

Figure 15.6 Avoid interpretations when describing an image (SOURCE https://www.insider.com/).

Alt text is plain text: it cannot include bold, italics, all caps, superscripts or subscripts, bulleted or numbered lists, maths symbols, etc. (Figure 15.7).

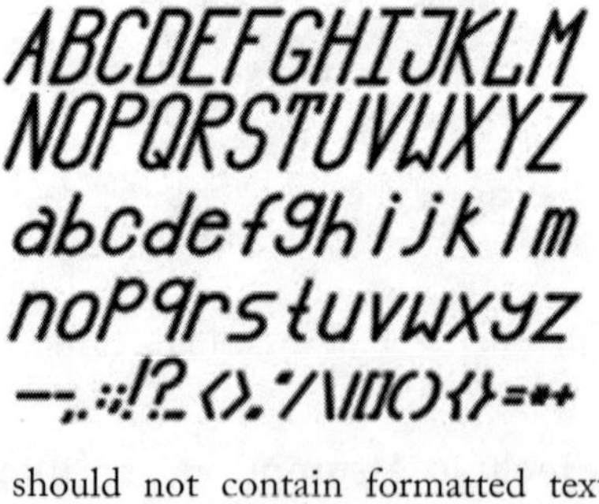

1234567890
ABCDEFGHIJKLM
NOPQRSTUVWXYZ
abcdefghijklm
nopqrstuvwxyz
-;.:;!?_<>.'/\|[]()(){}=*+

Figure 15.7 Alt text should not contain formatted text or special characters (SOURCE https://www.shutterstock.com/).

WHO CAN LEARN TO WRITE ALT TEXT

An alt text writer should possess good analytical skills, strong decision-making abilities, superlative English skills, subject-matter expertise, and sensitivity to the need of the audience.

Fresh graduates in science, technology, engineering, or medicine are considered ideal candidates by typesetting companies during recruitment because these fields witness continued research and publishing; the demand for alt text writers for books in these fields is much higher than that for books in the humanities and management-related subjects.

OPPORTUNITIES FOR ALT TEXT WRITERS

To learn alt text writing, you can either enrol for a formal training programme or join typesetting companies that recruit for the role of alt text writers after clearing any basic tests for proficiency in English.

Publishing

Onpaper Publishing Solutions, based in Pondicherry, India, an organization specializing in providing alt text services to various publishers, runs a specialized course on alt text writing, which teaches the basics of alt text and helps students learn and practice alt text for different kinds of images including illustrations, charts, graphs, photos, and cartoons. Free introductory classes are available at

- https://tinyurl.com/alt-txt0 (for class 1)
- https://tinyurl.com/alttextII (for class 2)
- https://tinyurl.com/alttextIII (for class 3).

Web accessibility

If you are a software developer and would like to explore a different career option, you can learn accessibility compliance and testing that is required for websites. Courses on web accessibility can be found on online learning platforms such as Udemy, Coursera, LinkedIn Learning, EdX, and others.

WHERE TO FIND WORK

Publishing

- At Onpaper: internship for freshers and full-time and freelancing jobs for experienced writers
- Other typesetting companies (full-time jobs and freelance options): Integra, Straive, Apex, NewGen, Codemantra, MPS, S4 Carlisle, Cenveo, Lumina Datamatics, etc.

Web accessibility

You can find positions such as accessibility engineer, accessibility quality analyst (QA), accessibility user interface (UI) developer, and accessibility consultant in top software companies, and you can explore freelance and full-time opportunities at job sites such as https://www.dice.com/, https://remotive.com/, https://weworkremotely.com/, https://remote.co/, https://wellfound.com/, https://www.upwork.com/, https://www.workingnomads.com/jobs, http://www1.jobespresso.co/, https://workinstartups.com/, https://www.naukri.com/, http://www.unicornhunt.io/, https://in.indeed.com/?r=us, https://www.flexjobs.com/, https://careesma.in/, https://hasjob.co/, and https://www.foundit.in/

CONCLUDING REMARKS

Accessibility is not only for people with disabilities but is useful to other people too in their day-to-day life although they seldom realize it. Navigational applications on smartphones (with the speaker switched on) so that you get appropriate directions in audio while you are driving are an accessibility product. Talking to your smart devices such as Google Home or Alexa, asking for weather or time, or instructing the device to play a piece of music or video are a few more examples. These examples show that accessibility helps all and not merely those with disabilities.

As the need for accessibility in all walks of our life continues to expand, new products and services continue to evolve rapidly. Given this scenario, taking up a career in accessibility will surely present you with a wide range of opportunities to explore.

Wishing you all the best in your career search!

FURTHER READING

Web Accessibility
https://webaim.org/techniques/alttext/

Web Content Accessibility Guidelines (WCAG)
https://www.w3.org/TR/WCAG21/

Digital Content Empowers Accessible Reading
https://inclusivepublishing.org/consumer/accessible-reading/

Screen Readers
https://www.w3schools.com/accessibility/accessibility_screen_readers.php

Visalakshy Loganathan (visalakshy.onpaper@gmail.com) is a copyeditor and an alt text writer with over two decades of experience in the publishing industry. In 2018, she organized the first-ever National Conclave for Editors, which was held in Chennai. She runs a company, Onpaper Publishing Solutions Pvt Ltd (www.onpaperpublishing.com), based in Puducherry, India, which specializes in editing and alt text writing services. Over the past 4 years, her team has generated alt text for more than 300,000 images for various publishers. Visalakshy runs a one-month certificate course in alt text writing (OMCCAT), and has trained more than a hundred students over the past two years and helped them in pursuing successful careers. She is currently cofounding a new startup (https://www.transpixed.pics/) in the United States, which will provide barrier-free content for websites and apps with the help of AI tech.

CHAPTER 16

The Art and Science of Indexing

P K Jayanthan

An index, also referred to as the back-of-the-book index, is a systematic arrangement of keywords and locators to help the reader find specific information in a book. The index acts as a concise and useful guide to information in, and adds value to, the book as a reference source.

An index is prepared after carefully reading, comprehending, and analysing the content of a publication to identify the terms that the user might search for – and is usually prepared simultaneously with, or after, the final proofreading. In recent times the importance of an index is increasingly being recognized.

Kinds of books indexed

Books with a reference value such as academic publications, travelogues, atlases, anthologies, conference proceedings, and higher-education books are usually indexed; fiction, children's books, and textbooks meant for primary or secondary schools are not.

Types of indexes

There are several types of indexes, such as an index of keywords, subjects, names, places, titles, and first lines, and one book may have multiple indexes (a keyword index and an index of names, for example) or a single comprehensive index of all indexable terms.

In a *keyword index*, specific keywords or phrases are selected as index terms.

In a *subject index*, the concept or idea is indexed. In such indexes, the exact keyword or phrase may not occur in the text but will have been inserted by the indexer. Here are a few examples of such additional terms.

> Jhabua civil district lies at the south-western edge of the state of Madhya Pradesh, India, bordering the states of Rajasthan and Gujarat.
>
> Index term: Jhabua, location of (The word 'location' is not mentioned in the passage.)

> The minister assured the people that unemployment, poverty, and food-and-water scarcity would be wiped out from the state and their standard of living would be improved.
>
> Index term: development, promise of

A *name index* consists of names of people and may accompany a review of literature, a collection of writings, a biography, or an autobiography.

A *geographical index* is prepared for atlases, gazetteers, maps, and travelogues, in which the names of places serve as index terms.

A *title index* consists of titles of books (in a book of literary criticism) or in a collection of literary works (collected poems or stories).

A *first-line index* is prepared for an anthology of poems or for a book of quotations, in which the first lines of the poems or quotations are used as index terms.

PREPARING AN INDEX

Parts of book to be included or excluded from the index

Apart from the main text, some elements from preliminary pages or front matter (foreword and preface, for example) and from end pages or end matter (glossary, appendices, etc.) are sometimes indexed.

A preface is a note from the author to the readers and usually does not contain much information on the topic of the book. In that case, the preface need not be indexed; however, if the preface does contain such information, the preface too should be indexed.

Dedications and acknowledgements need not be indexed.

An introduction, in most cases, contains significant information. Sometimes, it is as relevant as any other chapter in the book and, if so, must be indexed; if not, the introduction can be ignored while indexing.

Appendices or annexes should be indexed because they usually provide additional information.

Notes, other than those containing only references, should be indexed because they might contain additional information. References and a bibliography need not be indexed.

Parts of an index

A typical entry in an index has two parts: the index term, or keyword, and the locator. The keyword can be split into the main entry, a subentry, or a sub-subentry. The locator gives the location of the keyword in the text and in most cases consists of the number of the page on which the index term appears within the book; however, the locator can also be a paragraph number if each paragraph in the document is numbered, an article number or section number or a clause number, as in constitutions, bye-laws, or rules and regulations of associations, societies, etc.

Index entries reflect the author's perspectives or information and the reader's approach to the content.

Method of indexing

Before you begin, understand what the book to be indexed is about by reading the preface and other front matter, especially the table of contents, and get an overall idea of the book, to know how it has been conceived and presented by the author.

Complete and careful reading and understanding of the contents are necessary to prepare an index. Ideally the indexer should read the complete book once and should start selecting keywords only on second reading. However, lack of time may not allow the indexer to follow this approach. Publishers in general do not include the time for indexing while drawing up the schedule outlining the various stages in book production; fortunately, this practice is changing as more and more publishers realize the significance of the index and the value it adds to the book.

Before computers, keywords and locators were written on index cards, which were then manually sorted in alphabetical order and the index typed out on a typewriter. This process has now given way to computerized indexing.

Index can be prepared using either a hard copy or a soft copy, usually a file in PDF. On the hard copy, relevant words or phrases are marked with a highlighter or simply underlined. Sometimes one needs to mark two words or terms that are several lines apart and combine them into a single term. In such cases, the two are joined with a line, and when index entries are being typed, the two words are added as a single term. For a file in PDF, keywords are copied and pasted into a Word file; if the term is split between several lines, the whole portion is copied and pasted and the unwanted text deleted.

Passing references – when the text says little about the terms in question – need not be indexed. For example, the terms 'environmental degradation' or 'yearly rainfall' may occur in a book on India's foreign policy but are not indexed because the reader is unlikely to search for these terms in the index to that book.

However, there may be exceptions, and the author may want specific keywords or names to be included. For example, in a biography or autobiography, the author may insist on including the names of all those who are mentioned in the manuscript or in a travelogue, indexing every place name. In such cases, the terms are included regardless of their relevance – the indexer is not the final decision maker.

> The conference was organized by the local trade union and I noticed Mr Sharma, an old colleague, in the audience.

This may be the sole mention of this person, but index the name if the author insists.

> The meeting was organized at the Park Hotel in Connaught Place. On our way we passed through Sarojini Nagar.

Sarojini Nagar may have no relevance, but index the location if the author wants.

The title or the subtitle of the book, chapter titles, and name(s) of the author(s) or editor(s) in a book with different chapters contributed by different authors need not be indexed.

All keywords must always be nouns or pronouns and complete words. Compound or hyphenated words should not be split between a main entry and a subentry. Adjectives, even if they are nouns while standing alone, cannot be used as entries.

Correct	Incorrect	**Correct**	Incorrect	**Correct**	Incorrect
sunflower	sun	life-size	life	acetic acid	acid
sunlight	flower	life-threatening	size	acid rain	acetic
	light		threatening	acid solutions	rain
				sulphuric acid	solutions
					sulphuric

In tables and illustrations, keywords are taken from titles and captions. Keywords from within a table or an illustration need not be listed. In some cases, multiple keywords need to be selected from a single title or caption to cater to all possible searches by the reader.

> Title: Coal dispatches of various states (million tonnes): 1975/76 to 1999/2000
>
> Keyword: Coal dispatches from states

Do not include the names of individual states.

> Title: Raw coal feed and clean coal production of washeries
>
> Keywords: clean coal production of washeries
> raw coal feed of washeries
> washeries
> raw coal feed of
> clean coal production of

FORMATTING AND PRESENTING THE INDEX

Stage 1

Once a Word file is produced, either by typing or by copying and pasting the selected keywords and adding the corresponding locators, nearly one-third of the job is done. At this stage, a part of the index typically looks as shown below.

India became majoritarian 1
history of South Asian nations 1
India has not dabbled with constitutional majoritarianism 1
Indian Constitution 1
little resemblance to the values of the Constitution 2
India's route to majoritarianism 2
Hindutva ideology 2
word 'right' is used 2
'right' and 'left' mean 2
social conservatism 3
British conservatism 3

Stage 2

It is now time to edit, format, and complete the index. Each term should be very carefully read, understood, and arranged. Note that the normal order of words is reversed in an index: normally, the qualifier or the determiner comes before the noun being qualified (which is why G Norman Knight, an expert indexer, titled his book on indexing as *Indexing, the Art of: a guide to the indexing of books and periodicals*). With words in quotes, it may save some time if the first two or three letters of the word are added before it to help maintain the correct alphabetic order. In the example that follows, the letters 'rig' and 'lef' are inserted before the words 'right' and 'left' (in quotes) so that the entries fall in the correct order when the list is sorted automatically by Word. During such alphabetical sorting, Word places any non-alphabetic symbols and signs before alphabets. Here is how the entries now appear at the second stage.

India, majoritarianism of, 1
South Asian nations, history of, 1
India, constitutional majoritarianism in, 1
Indian Constitution, 1
Constitution, values of, 2
majoritarianism, in India, 2
Hindutva ideology, 2
rig'right', use of the word, 2, 4
rig'right', meaning of, 2, 3n1
lef'left', meaning of, 2
social conservatism, 3

Stage 3

An index may be alphabetized using the sorting feature available in Word. Once the list is correctly alphabetized, the extra letters added before some words may be deleted manually. Next, duplicate entries (the same keyword on different pages) and their respective locators are consolidated into a single entry and, where required, split into main entries and subentries. Finally, the appropriate individual letters are added as headings (the letters C, H, I, L, R, and S in the following example).

C
Constitution, values of, 2

H
Hindutva ideology, 2

I
India, majoritarianism in, 1, 2
  constitutional majoritarianism
  in, 1
Indian Constitution, 1

L
'left', meaning of, 2

R
'right'
  meaning of, 2, 3n1
  use of the word, 2, 4

S
social conservatism, 3
South Asian nations,
history of, 1

Styles

An index can be formatted in two styles, indented or run-on.

Indented style

Typically, each subentry must be indented one em space from the margin and run-on lines, by two em spaces. Sub-subentries must then be indented three em spaces and run-on lines in sub-subentries must be indented four em spaces. Because such indents of multiple depths are likely to confuse the reader, it may be a good idea to do away with the indents (em spaces) for run-on lines. Because this practice is user-friendly and looks better on the page, most publishers prefer the indented style. The disadvantage is that it takes up more space than the run-on style does. Even publishers who otherwise follow *The Chicago Manual of Style* prefer the indented style for indexing. This is how the indented style looks.

agricultural growth,
  Bihar, 213
  east India, 212
  Gujarat, 219–227

agriculture,
  capitalist development in, 221
  during Green Revolution, 224
  impact on water quality, 3

Run-on style

In the run-on style, the main entry, subentries, and sub-subentries are all placed one after the other without any indenting. A colon is added after the main entry, and subentries are separated by semicolons. Although this style saves considerable amount of space, it is harder to read and it takes longer to process the information presented in the index. *The Chicago Manual of Style* uses the run-on style.

agricultural growth: Bihar, 213; east India, 212; Gujarat, 219–227
agriculture: capitalist development in, 221; during Green Revolution, 224; impact on water quality, 3

GENERAL PRINCIPLES

- The acceptable length of an index is 2%–5% of the number of pages of the book. A fairly detailed index for a 100-page book will be about three pages long.
- It is generally accepted that no entry should have more than ten locators. It is frustrating to the reader to look up information on a single keyword across many pages. In such cases, subentries may be added to minimize the number of locators and to make the search easier for the reader. The ideal number of locators is about five (the repetition of page numbers from the main entry to its subentries should be avoided).
- All index entries, unless otherwise specified by the publisher, should always be in the lower case, except proper nouns and other terms that are always capitalized. Most publishers follow this style.

- It is advisable to set indexes ragged right (left aligned) although the book itself may be set fully justified. Setting the index justified introduces wide gaps between indexed terms, which looks awkward and disturbs the flow of reading.
- Any italics in the book (botanical names, for example) should be retained in the index as well. Even if the keyword is italicized only at its first occurrence in the text, the word should retain the italics in the index.
- Names of acts, bills, organizations, committees, and so on should be given in full in all instances, and not split into a main entry and a subentry, although several words are repeated (e.g., each of the many UN organizations will have a separate entry although many successive entries will begin with 'United Nations' as the first two words).
- If an abbreviation or acronym has more than one expanded form, and both are referred to in the book, the expanded forms should be given in parentheses for clarity along with their corresponding locators.
- If any subentry is carried over to the next page, the main entry should be repeated, followed by the word 'continued' or 'contd' within parentheses and italicized.

Locator formats

- Locators can be (a) page numbers (in majority of books), (b) paragraph numbers (in books where paragraphs are numbered), or (c) articles, schedules, sections, etc. (in constitutions, bye-laws, rules and regulations). In this chapter, page numbers are assumed to be the locators.
- If an index term is spread over more than one page, the initial page should be given as the locator.
- A keyword and its locator can be separated by one space, two spaces, or a comma and one space, depending on the style used

by the publisher. The generally accepted format is a comma and a space, as in *Handbook for Editors*, 24, 27.

- If a keyword appears on continuous pages, the first and the last pages can be mentioned separated by an en dash without space on either side, as in *Handbook for Editors*, 24–27.
- Follow the publishers' format for continuous pages. This can be given as 235–238 (without omitting, or eliding, any numerals) or as 235–38 or 235–8 (eliding redundant numerals). Although the generally accepted style is 235–38, other formats are also seen.
- If the keyword appears in a footnote or an endnote, insert the letter 'n' (for note) and the note number after the page number, as in *Handbook for Editors*, 234n5.
- Locators for titles of tables or captions to figures should ideally be distinguished by setting them in italics or in bold, but this makes them obtrusive. It is also likely that the table and the figure may have been mentioned on the same page; therefore, perhaps it is better to set the locator in plain type (neither italics nor bold).

Alphabetization

Alphabetization can be either letter by letter or word by word. The generally accepted style is letter by letter, or the dictionary style. Microsoft Word also uses this style while sorting entries alphabetically.

Letter by letter

Space and punctuation marks are ignored in sorting keywords using the letter-by-letter style.

Word by word

A space is considered as a character in sorting keywords using the word-by-word style, each word in an entry being sorted in succession and separately using the logic 'something before nothing' (a space is regarded as that something). If the first word is the same across multiple entries, the next word is considered while sorting. The following examples show how the same word appears in a different sequence depending on the style.

Letter by letter	**Word by word**
soul brother	soul brother
soul food	soul food
soulfulness	soul mate
soul mate	soul sister
soul sister	Soulfulness

The articles 'a', 'an', and 'the' are ignored while alphabetizing and placed after the noun in question, as in *Three Musketeers, The*; *Tale of Two Cities, A*; *Anthology of Poetry, An*.

Prepositions should be added where necessary to avoid ambiguity. For example, 'books' and 'children' as main and subentries may not tell the reader if they refer to books 'by' children, 'on' children, or 'for' children. The appropriate preposition should be added in such cases for clarity.

Cross-references

A cross-reference is a pointer to information from one place in a book to another place in the same book leading to additional information. Cross-references are generally preceded by *see*, *see also*, or *see under*, italicized and placed within parentheses. Cross-references should be meticulously checked to make sure that they do not lead to a dead end; for example, if the spelt-out form is used while indexing, as in ICF (*see* Indian Copyeditors Forum), the index should have an entry, with locators, for Indian Copyeditors Forum.

The first 'see' leads to an equivalent term, 'ICF' and 'Indian Copyeditors Forum' being the equivalent terms in the above example.

Such a situation occurs when both the terms are used in the book. In this example, 'ICF' will only be a cross-reference and will not have any locator after it; the spelt-out form, on the other hand, will be followed by appropriate locators. In addition, the abbreviated form is given, within parentheses, after the fully spelt-out form in the main entry, as in Indian Copyeditors Forum (ICF), 235.

'See also', on the other hand, suggests additional terms that are also used as indexing terms in their own right in that each is followed by appropriate locators, as in copyright (*see also* permission to reprint), 28, 55 and vice versa. Note that the cross-reference is placed before adding the locators.

'See under' is similar to 'see' but leads to a subentry in another location, as in *Discovery of India* (*see under* Nehru, Jawaharlal) (without locators). In this example, Nehru, Jawaharlal and its subentry *Discovery of India* will be followed by the appropriate locators.

INDEXING AS A CAREER

Although editing and proofreading are considered career options, indexing is not, at least at present in India, where indexing is yet to grow as a serious business. Full-time indexers are not employed in most publishing houses; most indexers are freelancers. On several occasions, an index is added merely as a tick in the box or out of compulsion. No serious professionalism or scientific thought goes into preparing indexes, indexers as a group having little say, although things are looking up of late for them.

By taking up indexing as a way to supplement your income, therefore, you stand nothing to lose and everything to gain. You can take up indexing if you (a) have a thorough knowledge of the language, (b) are able to comprehend the content, (c) have an analytical mind, (d) have an eye for detail, and most important, (e) are willing to take the mostly untravelled road. It will also help if you have somebody to guide you in the initial stages until you build a reputation and a reasonably good network of clients.

TRAINING COURSES IN INDEXING

There are several training courses for those who want to take up indexing as a career. Most of these, including online courses, are, however, offered by organizations outside India. Some prominent courses are briefly described here.

American Society for Indexing

The indexing training course conducted by the American Society for Indexing (https://www.asindexing.org) is open only to its members. The course is conducted online through a dedicated website and offers comprehensive theoretical and practical training. The course, in four modules to be completed in four years, offers information sharing from experienced indexers, practical exercises, and interactive sessions. The content is based on an international standard, namely *ISO 999:1996(en) Information and documentation — Guidelines for the content, organization and presentation of indexes* and *The Chicago Manual of Style*.

The society also offers a course on running indexing as a business, covering the essentials of starting and running a freelance business. The course content includes the basics, financial management and budgeting, contracts and negotiations with clients, subcontracting, and professional development. This course is open also to non-members.

University of California Berkeley

The University of California Berkeley's online indexing course (https://tinyurl.com/courseusa) is designed for prospective indexers and for writers who want to index their work.

Massive open online courses

'Indexing Books as a Career' (https://tinyurl.com/indexingcourse), one of the MOOCs, is an 8-hour introductory indexing course. It provides only an introduction to indexing and is not meant to be comprehensive.

The course, free of charge, is intended to educate those interested in indexing and working as indexers.

Indexing Boot Camp

The 'Indexing Boot Camp' (https://tinyurl.com/indexingcourseII) is intended for new indexers, for those who have taken the introductory courses, or for experienced indexers who want to polish their skills.

Institute of Certified Indexers

The Institute of Certified Indexers, in the United States (http://www.certifiedindexers.com/), provides indexers with professional certificates on passing the prescribed tests. Certificates are given to indexers who are skilled, familiar with indexing techniques, and able to produce high-quality indexes.

Society of Indexers

The Society of Indexers (https://www.indexers.org.uk), UK, runs an online course on indexing leading to accreditation and professional membership of the society. A high level of proficiency in English is required for the course, which is conducted by experienced indexers. The course includes indexing assignments, online group tutorials, and a student discussion forum and teaches basic principles and helps develop the skills for commercial indexing.

Australian and New Zealand Society of Indexers

The indexing courses conducted by the Australian and New Zealand Society of Indexers (https://www.anzsi.org) include theory classes, workshops, and online professional development sessions.

SOFTWARE FOR INDEXING

A good indexing software helps to some extent. Some features save a good amount of time, but do not replace human effort altogether.

The indexer, even while using a software package, has to read through carefully and understand the manuscript. And there is no getting away from meticulous editing of the index either, a task that requires considerable amount of time and effort.

Various software packages help in related tasks such as specifying terms that must be included or excluded, reversing the normal order – first name followed by last name – to last name followed by first name to help in alphabetic sorting, adding locators, adding subentries, writing the index terms as links to corresponding pages, writing the generated index to a new file in PDF or as a text file, alphabetizing entries, inserting and verifying cross-references, and ignoring conjunctions and prepositions while sorting alphabetically.

Although more and more features are being added to several indexing software packages as the technology continues to advance, human effort cannot be altogether done away with. Unless indexers read the whole manuscript, they cannot be sure that all relevant indexable terms are included in the index. It is okay to select words and then let the software prepare the index. For example, suppose 'assemble' is selected as an indexing term. The software indexes all the instances where 'assemble' and its variants appear. The software, however, cannot distinguish between constituent assembly, assembling a car, or people who assembled for a wedding – only human intelligence can decide which term is to be included and how. As long as a software does not 'think' and only 'obeys', human intervention will continue to be essential.

Here are links to a few popular indexing software packages (as of July 2021).

- CINDEX™
  https://www.scribendi.ai/cindex/
- PDF Index Generator
  https://www.pdfindexgenerator.com/

- Index manager
  https://index-manager.net/en/home/?v=c86ee0d9d7ed
- MACREX v9
  http://www.macrex.com/
- SKY Index (Professional Edition) ver. 7.0
  http://www.sky-software.com/

P K Jayanthan (jayanthan.pk@gmail.com) is an editor and book indexer. He holds a master's degree in English (Annamalai University) and another in mass communication (Kurukshetra University). He has edited as well as indexed books for many publishers and organizations including Sage, Oxford University Press, McGraw Hill India, the National Council of Applied Economic Research, Niyogi Books, TERI, and TERI Alumni Association. He has also given several presentations on book indexing.

APPENDIX

Courses on Copyediting

Manisha Upare Narisetty, Jasminder Maolankar, Nishtha Singh, and Smriti Chawla

I think that as an editor – to be a really good editor – you first of all have to be a really good listener.

Ellen Seligman[1]

The experience of becoming an editor varies from person to person: some develop the skill naturally; others have to acquire it. Editing, even copyediting, is more than merely fixing spelling, grammar, and punctuation errors. No matter what the form of publication, whether a trade book or an academic paper, fiction or non-fiction, or even poetry, the goal is always to make readers understand the words the same way the author intended them to be understood. Turning raw writing into a structured and finely tuned piece requires a unique skill set and comes under the umbrella term 'editing', which strives to make writing more impactful.

Most people become editors because of their passion for grammatical accuracy and language. For many, editing is also intuitive;

1 Medley (2016).

they understand the nuances of structure because they are attentive readers and enjoy working with text to make it flow and convey the right meaning. They have a knack for appropriate usage, whereas others have to hone their capabilities. In both cases, however, to be successful, one requires to develop editorial acumen and commitment to perfect written communication.

People enter the field of editing at various points in their careers. They pursue professional degrees in subjects such as literature, journalism, or mass communication and then segue into full-time editing. Some editors come from entirely different backgrounds but are intrigued by language as a whole. They may have years of experience in unrelated fields but, given their interest in the written word, they decide to become professional editors. They combine their expertise in a given field with editing and start afresh as editors.

Besides being proficient in grammar, spelling, and composition, an editor must possess effective communication tools for identifying the most appropriate structure, format, and content for each audience and purpose. Editors think on behalf of both the writer and the reader, as they provide a much-needed perspective from both ends. Besides being active readers, editors need to be active listeners – right from understanding what the publisher requires of a manuscript for eventual success in the market to comprehending the points the author is trying to make.

Increasingly, however, editors are expected to undergo formal training in editing and publishing, and training can range from a short course to a professional degree. Such training not only familiarizes the trainees with the aspects of the profession they may not be familiar with but also provides some objective measure to judge their progress.

Here are some benefits of undergoing formal training in editing:

- introduction to the basics of the field and editing different forms of writing

- exposure to different kinds of editing, namely structural, language, stylistic, and developmental
- opportunity to learn from the experiences of faculty and peers
- chance to develop a professional network
- interaction with and learning from mentors and alumni
- greater job prospects
- assessment of skills through building a portfolio
- access to resources

Whether one enrols in a course or learns on the job (or, eventually, both), ultimately what makes one a successful editor is the ability to improve with each project by learning and retaining the knowledge gained from experience.

In the past, one could be employed as an editor based on experience and a portfolio of work rather than certificates, which, in any case, were not easily acquired in countries such as India. Now, the scenario has changed: most of those who aspire to be editors have already undergone formal training and have a certificate or even a degree as evidence of such training. These credentials expand the possibility of international internships and higher-paying work. Being a professional editor is much like being a teacher or a researcher and hence one needs to learn the skills required to succeed in this profession.

Researching editing and publishing courses online often leaves one in a quandary: with so many options, how do we know which ones are genuine and which ones to choose to suit our needs and budget?

Both established editors and aspiring editors also struggle with a plethora of questions: Can an editing course replace on-the-job training or only supplement it? How do we vet these courses? Are these pre-recorded courses or does one get in-person feedback? Is ample practice material being provided? What additional resources are available to enhance our skill set? Is it better to invest in an expensive degree abroad or are domestic certificate courses enough to kick-start one's career? How long does the accreditation remain valid? Which version of English – US or UK – does the programme cover? Where does that leave other versions of English such as Australian and Indian? Which style guides are widely accepted?

To help answer these questions, we have compiled a list (see Table A.1 on p. 207) of editing and publishing courses available in different modes. These courses are listed based on information received from editors or authors who have taken these courses in the past, feedback received from members of the Indian Copyeditors Forum through a survey, and information on professional courses that ICF has access to.

The purpose of this chapter is to provide readers with information on as many available resources as possible.

EDITORIAL COURSES IN INDIA

During the COVID-19 pandemic, ICF organized virtual meets in which a range of topics related to editing and writing practices were discussed. It was noticed that quite a few members were primarily self-taught: they had learnt on the job or studied books on English grammar and manuscript development written mostly by foreign authors or experienced a mix of both at their workplace. This hybrid method of learning has resulted in a serious lack of uniformity, with little standardization, unlike that seen internationally.

This lack of standardization also leads to uncertainty on what is acceptable or recommended and what is not and raises many questions, some of which are discussed further in this chapter.

Potential editors, to further their understanding of the field and to receive formal training, undergo short-term courses from internationally acclaimed professional editorial entities, such as the Chartered Institute of Editing and Proofreading (www.ciep.uk) and ACES: the society for editing (www.aceseditors.org), or undergo specialized courses taught by various established members of the ICF. Many have also completed courses developed in India such as those conducted by the National

Book Trust (https://www.nbtindia.gov.in) and The Art of Copyediting (https://www.theartofcopyediting.com/ri-available-now).

Another set of problems faced by self-taught editors is related to the relevance of these international courses to Indian English and Indian publishing in English. This is particularly relevant as editing courses for English are still at a nascent stage here in India. Please note that we refer here only to Indian English publications: publishing in regional languages is well established and used to have a more robust ecosystem than their English counterpart until recently.

When Vivek Kumar, the founder of ICF, put forward the idea for this book, we began to assess the courses available in the market.

Some of the points we focused on included the following.

- What kind of professional training does the course offer? Is it a certificate course, a postgraduate degree, or a short-term introductory course?
- What is the duration of the course(s) and the approximate date of joining?
- Is the course still being offered?
- What is the channel (mode) for the course? Online or by correspondence or in person or a hybrid?
- Is it a private course started by someone certified through a professional body, such as the CIEP and ACES, or conducted by a university that specializes in the field?
- Are options available for specific topics such as technical writing, macros for editors, or book design?

CONCLUSION

During the various COVID-19 lockdowns, ICF started weekly seminars where everyone, irrespective of experience and seniority, could interact on a variety of topics ranging from understanding the nuances of Indian English to calculating your worth as a freelancer.

The recordings of these sessions are available on ICF's YouTube channel.

It was observed on multiple occasions that a majority of the more experienced professionals had branched out into editing as a second career and possessed minimum to no professional qualifications in the field. They had gained experience and honed their skills entirely on the job. This is contrary to the traditional view that it is mandatory to have some sort of formal education before venturing out to get a job.

How do we explain this contradiction? The reasons may be manyfold: the nature of the business, establishing practical skill sets, and foundation setting – all of which are at the core of mastering a subject.

Editing is after all a practical subject. Although there are established rules governing grammar and style, they can – and should – be tweaked depending on the material, especially in editing creative writing such as fiction. This judgement is developed only through practical training. However, as the adage goes, we need to master the rules before breaking them. Think of editing as learning a trade: formal training is still conducted in classrooms, but actual lessons sink in only at the workplace.

On the flip side, focusing solely on practical training can only take you so far. Real-world experience does go a long way, but it is the nitty-gritty, the minute details of an ever-evolving field, especially its more technical aspects, that a formal degree provides that is invaluable to the overall development of an editor. Plus, you develop contacts in the industry, which adds value to the ecosystem and contributes early on to establishing your career.

Editors, especially those working in a traditional publishing house, undertake diverse tasks. Sometimes, because of budgetary constraints, these roles overlap. Taking up relevant courses can nurture the appropriate skills and familiarize the participants with such tasks ahead of time. Even while offering internships, companies look for people with some prior knowledge, in which case this exposure through courses proves beneficial.

Finally, it is essential for effective copyeditors to have a broad understanding of the communication and publishing side of the industry. Copyeditors should also be able to work seamlessly with writers, publishers, web developers, designers, artists, photographers, project managers, printers, and other editors and should also be involved in – or at least should be aware of – acquisitions, manuscript and project development, research, structural editing, stylistic editing, rewriting, fact-checking, picture research, proofreading, indexing, layout, and production.

We have curated a comprehensive list of editorial courses available globally (see Table A.1 on p. 207). The list is accurate to our knowledge. We have categorized these courses by length (short-term or longer), type (certificate courses, postgraduate diplomas, or master-level courses), and channel (online or in person).

Note Some of these courses may have switched to online mode owing to the COVID-19 pandemic. The information is based on the course website current at the time of printing. As with all information, please cross-check with the concerned parties.

We hope this chapter provides some guidance to budding editors and helps kick-start their careers.

REFERENCE

Medley M. 2016. Celebrated editor Ellen Seligman dies. The Globe and Mail [Toronto], 25 March. https://tinyurl.com/ellenselgiman1

Manisha Upare Narisetty (manishaupare@gmail.com) has a master's degree in biotechnology and worked for a few years in research. Her love for reading and writing made her venture into freelance content writing. To supplement this, she underwent a course 'Essentials of Written English' from The Art of Copyediting. She loves to enable people and businesses to present their ideas to the world.

Jasminder Maolankar (minimaolankar@gmail.com) has been editing since 2009. She has a master's degree in business administration and has done courses in editing from Macmillan Publishing Services and The Art of Copyediting. She is also certified to offer training in IELTS and PTE (Pearson Test of English). After working with an award-winning agency for eight years, where she was Head of Copy Services, Jasminder now takes on freelance assignments to create, enhance, and edit content to professional standards.

Nishtha Singh (nishthasingh0@icloud.com) is an editor, writer, and researcher in the fields of architecture, broadcasting, ethics, and artificial intelligence. She has trained as an editor at the Seagull School of Publishing, Kolkata, and has a bachelor's degree in philosophy from the University of Delhi.

Smriti Chawla (smriti.chawla@hotmail.com) has a master's degree in journalism and a postgraduate degree in publishing from Queensland University of Technology, Australia. She worked with an independent publishing house in Mumbai before branching out to work independently. She specializes in fiction and poetry editing and is an experienced editor in the spiritual and self-help genres. She is a TEFL (Teaching English as a foreign language) and IELTS instructor and moonlights as a social media manager.

Table A.1 Formal courses in editing, publishing, and related fields/topics

No.	Title of the course, entity offering the course, and location of the entity	Mode of delivery	Link
Certificate courses			
1	Course in Book Design Seagull School of Publishing Kolkata, India	Regular	https://theseagullschool.wordpress.com/
2	Course in Editing Seagull School of Publishing Kolkata, India	Regular	https://theseagullschool.wordpress.com/
3	Multiple postgraduate courses Anna University Chennai, India	Online	https://www.annauniv.edu
4	Intensive Course for Editors in Publishing Institute of Book Publishing New Delhi, India	Regular or Online	ibpsterling.org
5	Online Course in Book Publishing National Book Trust New Delhi, India	Regular	https://www.nbtindia.gov.in
6	CSE Publication Certificate Program Council of Science Editors New York, USA	Online	http://www.councilscienceeditors.org/

Table A.1 Formal courses in editing, publishing, and related fields/topics (*continued*)

No.	Title of the course, entity offering the course, and location of the entity	Mode of delivery	Link
7	Editing certificate (continuing studies) Simon Fraser University Vancouver, Canada	Self-paced/ Online	http://www.sfu.ca/
8	Australian College Certificate of Editing and Publishing Australian College QED Pty Ltd Sydney, Australia	Online	https://www.australiancollege.edu.au/
9	Advanced Editing and Publishing Australian College QED Pty Ltd Sydney, Australia	Online	https://www.australiancollege.edu.au/
10	Applied Copyediting and Proofreading Australian College QED Pty Ltd Sydney, Australia	Online	https://www.australiancollege.edu.au/
11	Essential Skills Express Package certification American Medical Writers Association Rockville, USA	Online	https://www.amwa.org/

Table A.1 Formal courses in editing, publishing, and related fields/topics (*continued*)

No.	Title of the course, entity offering the course, and location of the entity	Mode of delivery	Link
12	Certificate in Editing University of Washington Seattle, USA	Online	https://www.pce.uw.edu/
13	Graduate Certificate of Editing and Publishing University of Southern Queensland Towoomba, Australia	Regular	https://usq.edu.au/
14	Graduate Diploma of Editing and Publishing University of Southern Queensland Towoomba, Australia	Regular	https://usq.edu.au/
15	Medical Writing and Editing University of Chicago Graham School Chicago, USA	Online	https://grahamschool.uchicago.edu/
16	Certificate in Professional Copyediting, Proofreading and Fact-checking NYU School of Professional Studies New York, USA	Online	https://www.sps.nyu.edu/

Table A.1 Formal courses in editing, publishing, and related fields/topics (*continued*)

No.	Title of the course, entity offering the course, and location of the entity	Mode of delivery	Link
17	Graduate Certificate of Editing and Electronic Publishing Macquire University Sydney, Australia	Online	https://courses.mq.edu.au/
18	A Grammar Refresher Grammar Lion USA	Online	https://www.grammar-lion.com/
19	Poynter ACES Certificate in Editing ACES with Poynter Institute's News University St. Petersburg, USA	Online	https://www.poynter.org/
20	Proofreading and Copyediting with *The Chicago Manual of Style* Editorial Freelancers Association New York, USA	Online	https://www.the-efa.org/
21	Manuscript Assessment and Development Editing in Fiction Renee Otmar Consultancy Geelong, Australia	Online	https://reneeotmar.com.au/

Table A.1 Formal courses in editing, publishing, and related fields/topics (*continued*)

No.	Title of the course, entity offering the course, and location of the entity	Mode of delivery	Link
22	Foundation for making books inclusive Beth Cox Inclusion and Equity Consultant Salisbury, UK	Online	www.bethcox.co.uk/
Postgraduate diploma or certificate or degree courses			
1	PG Certificate Course in Editing and Publishing at the School of Cultural Texts and Records Jadavpur University Kolkata, India	Regular	http://editpub.blogspot.com
2	PG Diploma in Book Publishing Indira Gandhi National Open University (IGNOU) New Delhi, India	Distance	http://www.ignou.ac.in/
3	PG Diploma in Book Publishing Studies University of Calcutta Kolkata, India	Regular	http://www.caluniv.ac.in/
4	Graduate Diploma in Publishing Te Euaha NZ Institute of Creativity Te Aro, New Zealand	Regular	https://teauaha.com/

Table A.1 Formal courses in editing, publishing, and related fields/topics (*continued*)

No.	Title of the course, entity offering the course, and location of the entity	Mode of delivery	Link
5	DPI Certificate in Publishing Denver Publishing Institute University of Denver Denver, USA	Regular	https://liberalarts.du.edu/
6	Masters in Publishing Simon Fraser University British Columbia, Canada	Regular	https://publishing.sfu.ca/
7	Undergraduate Minor in Print and Digital Publishing Simon Fraser University British Columbia, Canada	Regular	https://publishing.sfu.ca/
8	Master of Science in Technical Communication Northeastern University San Francisco San Francisco, USA	Online	https://bayarea.northeastern.edu/
9	MS in Publishing: Digital and Print Media NYU School of Professional Studies New York, USA	Regular	https://www.sps.nyu.edu/

Table A.1 Formal courses in editing, publishing, and related fields/topics (*continued*)

No.	Title of the course, entity offering the course, and location of the entity	Mode of delivery	Link
10	The Club Ed Certificate in Developmental Editing of Fiction Editing Program + multiple courses Club Ed	Self-paced and Instructor-led, online	https://www.clubedfreelancers.com/
11	Certificate in Editing University of Washington Seattle, USA	Online	https://www.pce.uw.edu/
12	Business Writing workshops Colbourne Communications Toronto, Canada	Online/ In-person	www.colcomm.ca
Short-term online courses			
1	Editing 101 April Michelle Davis	Online	https://editorialinspirations.com/
2	Grammar Refresher courses April Michelle Davis	Online	https://editorialinspirations.com/
3	Indexing 101 April Michelle Davis	Online	https://editorialinspirations.com/
4	Macros 101 April Michelle Davis	Online	https://editorialinspirations.com/

Table A.1 Formal courses in editing, publishing, and related fields/topics (*continued*)

No.	Title of the course, entity offering the course, and location of the entity	Mode of delivery	Link
5	Writing courses Edex.org	Online	https://www.edx.org/
6	References Chartered Institute of Editing and Proofreading London, UK	Online	https://www.ciep.uk/
7	Copyediting UC San Diego Extension San Diego, USA	Online	http://extension.ucsd.edu/
8	Copyediting I UC San Diego Extension San Diego, USA	Online	http://extension.ucsd.edu/
9	Grammar, Mechanics and Usage for Editors UC Berkley Extension Berkley, USA	Online	https://extension.berkeley.edu/
10	Editorial workshops (Introduction, Intermediate, Advanced) UC Berkley Extension Berkley, USA	Online	https://extension.berkeley.edu/

Table A.1 Formal courses in editing, publishing, and related fields/topics (*continued*)

No.	Title of the course, entity offering the course, and location of the entity	Mode of delivery	Link
11	Multiple editorial courses Anantharaman Venkataraman India (Global site)	Online	https://theartofcopyediting.com/
12	Multiple editorial courses Anantharaman Venkataraman India (Indian site)	Online	https://www.theartofcopyediting.com/ri-available-now
13	Multiple editorial courses The Publishing Training Centre London, UK	Online	https://www.publishingtrainingcentre.co.uk/
14	Education your way American Medical Writers Association Rockville, USA	Self-study	https://www.amwa.org/
15	Online Learning: several courses on editing, tables and graphs, using Microsoft etc. American Medical Writers Association Rockville, USA	Self-study	https://www.amwa.org/

Table A.1 Formal courses in editing, publishing, and related fields/topics (*continued*)

No.	Title of the course, entity offering the course, and location of the entity	Mode of delivery	Link
16	Editing and Proofreading series University of Alberta Edmonton, Canada	Regular	https://ext.ualberta.ca/
17	Introduction to Technical Writing Society for Technical Communication Fairfax, USA	Online	https://www.stc.org/
18	Publishing Talks, Lectures and Seminars Simon Fraser University British Columbia, Canada	Online	https://publishing.sfu.ca/
19	Copy and Stylistic Editing I The Chang School of Continuing Education Ryerson University Toronto, Canada	Online	https://continuing.ryerson.ca/
20	Copy and Stylistic Editing II The Chang School of Continuing Education Ryerson University Toronto, Canada	Online	https://continuing.ryerson.ca/

Table A.1 Formal courses in editing, publishing, and related fields/topics (*continued*)

No.	Title of the course, entity offering the course, and location of the entity	Mode of delivery	Link
21	Digital Publishing and Production The Chang School of Continuing Education Ryerson University Toronto, Canada	Online	https://continuing.ryerson.ca/
22	Editing Books for Children and Teens The Chang School of Continuing Education Ryerson University Toronto, Canada	Online	https://continuing.ryerson.ca/
23	Editing Recipes and Cookbooks The Chang School of Continuing Education Ryerson University Toronto, Canada	Online	https://continuing.ryerson.ca/
24	Practical Grammar and Punctuation The Chang School of Continuing Education Ryerson University Toronto, Canada	Online	https://continuing.ryerson.ca/

Table A.1 Formal courses in editing, publishing, and related fields/topics (*continued*)

No.	Title of the course, entity offering the course, and location of the entity	Mode of delivery	Link
25	Proofreading for Books, Journals and Reports The Chang School of Continuing Education Ryerson University Toronto, Canada	Online	https://continuing.ryerson.ca/
26	Editing in Academic and Professional Contexts Queen's University, Kingston, Canada	Regular	https://www.queensu.ca/
27	Editorial Skills for All The Publishing Training Centre London, UK	Regular	https://www.publishingtrainingcentre.co.uk/
28	Introduction to Editorial Skills: Copy-editing and Proofreading The Publishing Training Centre London, UK	Online	https://www.publishingtrainingcentre.co.uk/
29	Progress in Editorial Skills: Copy-editing and Proofreading The Publishing Training Centre London, UK	Online	https://www.publishingtrainingcentre.co.uk/

Table A.1 Formal courses in editing, publishing, and related fields/topics (*continued*)

No.	Title of the course, entity offering the course, and location of the entity	Mode of delivery	Link
30	Rewriting and Substantive Editing (Non-Fiction) The Publishing Training Centre London, UK	Online	https://www.publishingtrainingcentre.co.uk/
31	Inclusive Editing Media Bistro	Online	https://www.mediabistro.com/
32	Multiple short courses Media Bistro	Online	https://www.mediabistro.com/
33	Multiple short courses Editorial Freelancers Association New York, USA	Online	https://www.the-efa.org/
34	Multiple short courses Editorial Arts Academy Montpelier, USA	Online	https://editorialartsacademy.com/
35	Multiple short courses Vijay Nicole Chennai, India	Regular	http://vijaynicole.co.in/
36	Multiple courses Liminal Pages Bishop's Stortford, UK	Self-study and Tutored	https://www.liminalpages.com/
37	Multiple short courses Colborne Communications Toronto, Canada	Starting online soon	http://colcomm.ca/

Table A.1 Formal courses in editing, publishing, and related fields/topics (*continued*)

No.	Title of the course, entity offering the course, and location of the entity	Mode of delivery	Link
38	Multiple short courses Page Two Editorial Annapolis, USA	Regular	https://pagetwoeditorial.com/
39	Business and Marketing Skills for Editors Edit Boost Canberra, Australia	Online/ Phone	https://www.editboost.com/
40	Macros for Editors Paul Beverley Norwich, UK	Flexible	http://archivepub.co.uk/
41	Children's books, bookmapping, marketing your services Heidi Fiedler Boxborough, USA	Online	https://www.helloheidifiedler.com/
42	Introduction to Professional Academic Editing Ideas on Fire Palmyra, USA	Online	https://ideasonfire.net/
43	Essentials of Language Editing Editor's Essentials Chennai, India	Online	https://editorsessentials.com
44	Editorial courses Archer Editorial Training Kingston, Canada	Online	www.archer-editorial-training.teachable.com

Table A.1 Formal courses in editing, publishing, and related fields/topics (*continued*)

No.	Title of the course, entity offering the course, and location of the entity	Mode of delivery	Link
45	Developmental editing for academics Manuscript Works Los Angeles, California	Online	https://courses.manuscriptworks.com/
46	Training courses for editors and writers Louise Harnby, Fiction editor and proofreader England, UK	Online	www.louiseharnbyproofreader.com
47	Structural editing for Editors Nicola O'Shea editing services and training	Online	www.nicolaoshea.com
48	Editing courses Pikko's School of Wordcraft and Editing Honolulu, USA	Online	https://courses.pikkoshouse.com/
49	Proofreading and business development courses Denise Cowle Editor and Proofreader Greater Glasgow Area, Scotland, UK	Online	www.denisecowleeditorial.com
50	Grammar refresher courses Grammar Lion New York, USA	Online	www.grammar-lion.com

Table A.1 Formal courses in editing, publishing, and related fields/topics (*continued*)

No.	Title of the course, entity offering the course, and location of the entity	Mode of delivery	Link
51	Various courses Tanya Gold Boston, USA	Online	www.tanyagold.com
52	Editing tools workshops Cadman Training Services Bellingen, Australia	Online	www.cadmantraining.com

Glossary

Rajeswari Krithivasan

Academic editing: a process in which a subject expert prepares for publication documents that are meant for schools, colleges, universities, and other educational institutions. Such editing may also be undertaken for training manuals and other instructional documents.

Alt text (alternative text): also known as 'alt attributes' or 'alt descriptions', alt text is the text given along with images that is read out aloud by screen readers to assist visually impaired users in navigating digital documents.

Anthology: literally meaning a collection of flowers, is a book that contains work on a particular subject (mostly literary pieces like poems and stories) by different authors.

Appendix: extra information provided at the end of the book but not part of the main text. Although appendixes contain useful additional information, the book is complete even without that information. See also Supplement.

Author query (abbreviated to AQ): an essential part of the editorial process in which a copyeditor or a proofreader ascertains from authors whether the suggested changes to the manuscript are acceptable to them.

Back matter: the material that is given after the main text of a manuscript or a book and consisting of appendixes, endnotes, glossary, bibliography, and index.

Bias-free language: using words and phrases that do not demean or exclude people based on their age, sex, race, ethnicity, social class, or physical or mental traits; for example, 'chairperson' is preferred to 'chairman' and 'visually challenged' to 'blind'.

Bibliography: a collection of references to works (such as books and articles) on a specific topic; appears as part of the back matter of a book, report, online presentation, or a research paper. Matter under the heading 'Works cited' or 'References' consists only of sources cited or referred to in the main document, whereas a bibliography may include items not specifically cited or referred to.

Blind review (also blind refereeing): evaluating a manuscript by masking the name of the author so that the name or affiliation of the author does not affect the judgement of the publisher.

Byline: the line at the beginning or at the end of a news item or magazine article that mentions the writer's name.

Callout: a note added in the manuscript to indicate where a figure, a table, or any other item of artwork is to be placed. A copyeditor has to ensure that proper callouts are added in the manuscript.

Checklist: a comprehensive list of checks prepared by a copyeditor that need to be carried out while editing a manuscript.

Citation: in research materials, citations are pointers to sources (other texts) an author has used to substantiate the author's views. Each citation in text should have a corresponding reference at the end of the text.

Content editing (also known as substantive editing, comprehensive editing, macro editing, or heavy editing): an editing process that checks for organization, continuity, content, visual design, and comprehensibility.

Copy: an unedited manuscript that is to be typeset.

Copyediting (also copy editing): the process of preparing a document for formal publication, whether print or electronic. Copyediting is carried out to ensure that errors related to style, usage, punctuation, consistency, and so on are corrected.

Copyeditor (also copy editor): a person who edits a manuscript to remove errors, ambiguities, and inconsistencies of spelling, usage, and so on.

Copyright permission: the process of getting approval from the copyright owner of the original work to use it in another work.

Corrigendum (also addendum or erratum): a document or sheet of paper that contains corrected versions of errors in printed material; the document is bound or attached to the book before it is distributed.

Cover design: the layout, text, and format used for designing the visual appearance of the cover of a printed document.

Credit line: a statement that acknowledges the source of an illustration.

Cross-reference (also x-ref): a reference to pertinent information given at another place in the same document.

Desktop publishing (or DTP): formatting and combining text, tabulated data, illustrations, and other visual elements in a document using a desktop computer. Desktop publishing refers to small-scale publishing, unlike mainstream publishing, which uses larger machines and usually offset printing.

Developmental editing: a collaborative process that involves making substantial changes to a manuscript. The editor suggests changes in language, content, structure, development of topics or characters, amount of focus on particular aspects of the content, and so on (unlike copyediting, which focuses on the micro level).

DOI: an abbreviation for Digital Object Identifier, a unique numeric string (e.g. 10.1086/597483) assigned to a publication or other unit of intellectual property. The identifier is usually provided in references, typically preceded by https://doi.org/, for locating an object easily on the internet.

E-book: short for electronic book, the term refers to a book published in electronic format so that the contents can be read on a computer or a mobile phone.

Edited volume: a collection of articles on a particular topic in a single book contributed by different authors.

Edition: a particular version of a book that is printed.

Endnote: information added at the end of a chapter or a book that may include references, additional explanation for the main text, or a comment.

Extract (also block quote): material that is quoted from another book, article, or any other published material.

Fact-checking: the process of checking that all factual details provided by the author are accurate.

Formatting: arranging and organizing the content of a page with regard to font, spacing, and so on, especially on a computer.

Freelance: to provide services based on the work quantified by the number of words, pages, hours, job, and so on, instead of working as a regular salaried employee.

Front matter: the contents before the main text comprising parts such as the title page, copyright page, dedication, table of contents, lists of figures and tables, foreword, preface and acknowledgements. Also called prelims.

Galley: the first proof of typeset matter that is uncut and unbound and usually running to multiple pages.

Gender bias: refers to the preference shown to a particular gender while referring to a person in the text. To avoid gender bias, the pronoun 'they' has been accepted as a singular pronoun by most publishers.

Glossary: a list of terms arranged in alphabetical order at the end of a book containing definitions of important terms used in the text relating to a specific subject.

Hard copy: textual material that appears on paper. See also Soft copy.

Harvard style: a popular style used for in-text citations using the author–date system (e.g. Sen 2022). See also Vancouver style.

Header: a line repeated at the top of each page of a document. Also called running head.

House style: collection of certain rules and procedures regarding word choice, tone, specific grammar and punctuation issues, and product names to guide those involved in the editorial process to maintain uniformity in the style of various publications from the same publisher and within the parts of the same publication.

Index: an alphabetized list of names, places, topics, authors, and so on along with page numbers, usually at the end of a book, that enables a reader to easily locate a specific bit of information within the book.

Indexing: the process of preparing and compiling an index.

LaTeX: a software package used for typesetting technical documents that require precise placement of type (e.g. complex equations and formulae).

Line break: inserting a break in a line to accommodate the line within the width of a display area.

Macros (short for macroinstructions): a set of instructions in a word processor that can perform a sequence of operations to facilitate repetitive tasks.

Managing editor: a member of the editorial team who directly supervises the day-to-day operations of a publication, hires and supervises freelancers to do those tasks, and reports to the editor-in-chief.

Manuscript (often abbreviated to MS): the original unpublished work of an author before it is processed, typeset, and published.

Markup: the process of adding editing instructions using tags or codes (such as HTML) on a copy or layout.

Monograph: a long article or a short book written by specialists for other specialists on a single subject or single aspect of a subject. A monograph need not necessarily be written by a single author.

Non-breaking space: a narrow space that is used to avoid separating a number (quantity) from its unit or to ensure that two or more elements always appear together (in the same line of text).

Open-access publishing: publishing scholarly materials that are available to readers for free (i.e. without a subscription).

Peer-review process: the process initiated and managed by either a publisher or an editor to determine the scholarly quality of a book or an article. The process usually involves two or more subject experts commenting on the quality of the work and assessing whether it is fit for publication.

Prepress: the process of creating a print layout and performing a number of checks before the material is printed.

Preprint: a version of an article published online in advance of formal publication for marketing purposes or for wider dissemination.

Proofreading: the process of carefully examining typeset matter for finding and correcting any mistakes in the text to make sure that there are no omissions, missing pages, misalignment, and awkward word or page breaks.

Public domain: a work is said to be in public domain if it can be accessed and reproduced legally without the need for obtaining permission of the copyright owner.

Publication agreement: a contract between an author and a publisher that includes details of copyright ownership, duties of the author and publisher, and the terms and conditions for reproducing and distributing the book.

Publishing ethics: rules that need to be followed while using the results of previously published research or scholarly work.

Quotation: quoted material from a work that is already published.

Recto: a right-hand page. See also Verso.

References: any published or unpublished sources that are used to substantiate the facts or information provided in the text.

Reprint (or impression): publishing already published material in a different format that may or may not incorporate corrections. See also Edition.

Run on (also run in): to continue on the same line without a break.

Serial comma (also Oxford comma): the comma that precedes 'and' or 'or' before the last item in a series of three or more items (e.g. one, two, and three).

Short title: abbreviated title of a reference used in a note or citation to refer to the work once again after its full title has been given on its first appearance.

Soft copy: an electronic copy of a manuscript. See also Hard copy.

Soft hyphen (also optional hyphen): if a word needs to be broken at the end of a line, a hyphen is added by the word processor to split the word. The hyphen disappears if, because of any changes to text, the word is not split.

Spellcheck: a feature provided in a computer program that is used to check for spelling errors.

Stet: the instruction not to implement a change suggested by the copyeditor or proofreader.

Structural editing: a step in editing that suggests changes to the author regarding reorganizing the structure and adding or deleting content.

Style guide/manual: a document containing a set of instructions that need to be followed while writing, formatting, and designing the text that needs to be published (e.g. *The Economist Style Guide*, *The Chicago Manual of Style*, *The Times Style Guide* and *The New York Times Manual of Style and Usage*).

Style sheet: a record maintained by a copyeditor to note the treatment of spelling, hyphenation, capitalization, and so on followed for a particular job while copyediting.

Supplement: additional material in the book that is published separately for providing corrections or presenting updated information. See also Appendix.

Suspended hyphen: When a hyphenated adjective is repeated in a sentence, instead of repeating the word, a hyphen is used to indicate the connection to the last word. For example, long- or short-term policy and 3-, 6-, and 9-year-old children.

Typesetting: converting a copyedited document into page proofs by applying specified style and formatting based on the specifications given by the designer and the requirements of the publisher.

URL (abbreviated form of uniform resource locator): the web address that is used to find a web page or document available online.

Vancouver style: a citation style that uses numbers for in-text citations. See also Harvard style.

Verso: a left-hand page. See also Recto.

Further Reading and Sources of Information

Kinjal Patel, Kaneez Razavi, and
Rajeswari Krithivasan

Style guides

The ACS Style Guide, 3rd edn. The American Chemical Society. 2006. 448 pp.

American Medical Association Manual of Style, 11th edn. Oxford University Press. The JAMA Network Editors. 2020. 1256 pp.

The Associated Press Stylebook 2022–2024, 56th edn. The Associated Press. 2022. 1518 pp.

The Cambridge Guide to Australian English Usage, 2nd edn. Cambridge University Press. Peters P. 2007. 924 pp.

The Chicago Manual of Style, 17th edn. The University of Chicago Press Editorial Staff. 2017. 1184 pp.

The Columbia Guide to Online Style, 2nd edn. Columbia University Press. Walker J and Taylor T. 2004. 260 pp.

MLA Handbook for Writers of Research Papers, 6th edn. Gibaldi J. 2003. 360 pp.

MLA Style Manual and Guide to Scholarly Publishing, 3rd edn. Modern Language Association of America. 2008. 336 pp.

New Hart's Rules, 2nd edn. Oxford University Press. Waddingham A. 2014. 474 pp.

The New York Times Manual of Style and Usage, 5th edn. Siegal A M and Connolly W G. 2015. 368 pp.

The Oxford Style Manual. Oxford University Press. Ritter R M. 2003. 1033 pp.

Publication Manual of the American Psychological Association, 7th edn. American Psychological Association. 2019. 428 pp.

SBL Handbook of Style, 2nd edn. Society of Biblical Literature. 2014. 368 pp.

Books

Buky E, Schwartz M, and Einsohn A. 2019. *The Copyeditor's Workbook: exercises and tips for honing your editorial judgment.* Berkeley, CA: University of California Press. 384 pp.

Dreyer B. 2019. *Dreyer's English: an utterly correct guide to clarity and style*. New York: Random House. 292 pp.

Einsohn A and Schwartz M. 2019. *The Copyeditor's Handbook: a guide for book publishing and corporate communications*, 4th edn. Berkeley, CA: University of California Press. 584 pp.

Brooks B S and Pinson J L. 2018. *The Art of Editing in the Age of Convergence*. New York: Routledge. 420 pp.

Ginna P (ed.). 2017. *What Editors Do: the art, craft, and business of book editing*. Chicago: The University of Chicago Press. 310 pp.

Reeder E. 2016. *Three Types of Editors: developmental editors, copyeditors, and substantive editors*. New York: Editorial Freelancers Association. 46 pp.

Saller C F. 2016. *The Subversive Copy Editor*. 2nd edn. Chicago: The University of Chicago Press. 200 pp.

Johanson B. 2010. *Daily Grammar Lessons*. Taylorsville, UT: Word Place. 44 pp.

Israel S. 2009. *A Career in Book Publishing*, 3rd edn. New Delhi: National Book Trust. 159 pp.

Noton S. 2009. *Developmental Editing: a handbook for freelancers, authors and publishers*. Chicago: The University of Chicago Press. 252 pp.

Gilad S. 2007. *Copyediting and Proofreading for Dummies*. Hoboken, NJ: Wiley. 364 pp.

Smith R F and O'Connell L M. 2007. *Editing Today*, 2nd edn. Hoboken, NJ: Wiley-Blackwell. 260 pp.

Butcher J, Drake C, and Leach M. 2006. *Butcher's Copy-editing: the Cambridge handbook for editors, copy-editors and proofreaders*, 4th edn. Cambridge, England: Cambridge University Press. 544 pp.

Sullivan K D and Eggleston M. 2006. *The McGraw-Hill Desk Reference for Editors, Writers, and Proofreaders*. New York: McGraw-Hill. 238 pp.

Sharada Prasad H Y et al. 2004. *Editors on Editing*. New Delhi: National Book Trust. 109 pp.

Joshi Y. 2003. *Communicating in Style*. New Delhi: The Energy and Resources Institute. 250 pp.

Truss L. 2003. *Eats, Shoots & Leaves*. New York: Gotham Books. 210 pp.

Feld E. 2002. *Comma Sense*. Coral Gables, FL: Mango Publishing. 284 pp.

Stainton E M. 2002. *The Fine Art of Copyediting*, 2nd edn. New York: Columbia University Press. 160 pp.

Judd K. 2001. *Copyediting: a practical guide*, 3rd edn. Menlo Park, CA: Crisp Publications. 304 pp.

Cook C K. 1985. *Line by Line: how to edit your own writing.* Boston, MA: Houghton Mifflin Harcourt. 220 pp.

Journal articles

LaPinte J. 2023. Copyediting in 2023: what has changed? *Science Editor* **46** (1). https://tinyurl.com/copychange2023

Regala J. 2023. LinkedIn: an effective global publishing network at your fingertips. *Science Editor* **46** (1). https://tinyurl.com/cseedit0

Yoon J, Kim N, and Chung E. 2023. Characteristics of scholarly journals published in non-English-speaking countries: an analysis of library and information science SCOPUS journals. *Learned Publishing* **36**: 14–24. https://doi.org/10.1002/leap.1520

Christiansen S L. 2022. Writing the "right" words. *Science Editor* **45**: 37–38. https://doi.org/10.36591/SE-D-4501-37

Klika K D. 2022. Text recycling and excessive attribution: a pragmatic perspective. *Journal of Scholarly Publishing* **53**: 177–191.

Rowland F. 2022. The peer-review process. *Learned Publishing* **15**: 247–258. https://onlinelibrary.wiley.com/doi/10.1087/095315102760319206

Springer M. 2022. Current guidance on inclusive language for medical and science journals. *Science Editor* **45**: 136–138. https://tinyurl.com/cseedit1

Brown S A. 2021. The role of the editor of an academic publication blog. *Journal of Scholarly Publishing* **52**: 199–211.

Cary M. 2021. Standardizing terminology for text recycling in research writing. *Learned Publishing* **34**: 370–378. https://onlinelibrary.wiley.com/doi/10.1002/leap.1372

Smart P. 2020a. Dealing with difficult authors. *European Science Editing* **46**: e52201. https://doi.org/10.3897/ese.2020.e52201

Smart P. 2020b. Publishing during pandemic: innovation, collaboration, and change. *Learned Publishing* **33**: 194–197.

Ufnalska S and Terry A. 2020. Proposed universal framework for more user-friendly author instructions. *European Science Editing* **46**: e53477. https://doi.org/10.3897/ese.2020.e53477

Wheatley D. 2020. The "ize" have it – reflections on spelling and its rules. *European Science Editing* **46**: e59855. https://doi.org/10.3897/ese.2020.e59855

Roth R A. 2019. Understanding the importance of copyediting in peer-reviewed manuscripts. *Science Editor* **42**: 51–54. https://tinyurl.com/csesciedit

Mahaliyanaarachchi R P. 2017. Copy editing of the journal articles. *Journal of Agricultural Sciences – Sri Lanka* **12**. https://doi.org/10.4038/jas.v12i1.8199

Albert N G, Wharton R M, and Brand A. 2016. Demographics of scholarly publishing and communication professionals. *Learned Publishing* **29**: 97–101.

Elizabeth W. 2014. Defining and responding to plagiarism. *Learned Publishing* **27**: 33–42. https://onlinelibrary.wiley.com/doi/10.1087/20140105

King M. 2014. Will automated copy editors replace human ones? *American Journalism Review*. https://ajr.org/2014/04/15/copy-editors-in-digital-world/

Ufnalska S B and Polderman A K S. 2014. Golden rules for scholarly journal editors. *European Science Editing* **40**: 65. https://tinyurl.com/cseedit2

Pasco A H. 2009. Should graduate students publish? *Journal of Scholarly Publishing* **40**: 231–240.

Wates E and Campbell R. 2007. Author's version vs. publisher's version: an analysis of the copy-editing function. *Learned Publishing* **20**: 121–129. https://doi.org/10.1087/174148507X185090.

Iverson C. 2004. "Copy editor" vs. "manuscript editor" vs ... venturing onto the minefield of titles. *Science Editor* **27**: 39–41.

Newsletters

All About Book Publishing
http://www.allaboutbookpublishing.com/

Bacon Editing: Expert English language editing for scientists
http://baconediting.com

Editorial Arts Academy
https://editorialartsacademy.com/

Blog posts

CE-L Subscribers' Blogs: Info on copyediting blogs
http://www.copyediting-l.info/blogs.html

Feedly: Best editing blogs and websites
https://feedly.com/i/top/editing-blogs

Articles on copyediting

American Press Institute: Study shows the value of copy editing
https://tinyurl.com/valuecopy

Copify: How to become a copyeditor
https://blog.copify.com/post/how-to-become-a-copy-editor

Grammarly: Copy editing vs. proofreading: what's the difference?
https://tinyurl.com/copyprofdif

Kotobee: What you need to know about copyediting
https://blog.kotobee.com/copyediting/

Louise Harnby: The editing blog
https://www.louiseharnbyproofreader.com/blog/category/fiction-editing/2

Marketing Sherpa: Marketing 101: copywriting vs. copy editing vs. content writing
https://tinyurl.com/copycontentt

Master Class: How to copy edit: A guide to copy editing everything
https://www.masterclass.com/articles/a-guide-to-copy-editing-everything

Reedsy Blog: How to become a copy editor: 6 steps to book your first clients
https://blog.reedsy.com/freelancer/how-to-become-a-copy-editor/

Skill Share: Copy editing: build a career in editing
https://www.skillshare.com/blog/copy-editing-build-a-career-in-editing/

The Starr Conspiracy: 4 writing and editing blogs you should bookmark now
https://tinyurl.com/editblog4

Wikipedia: Copy editing
https://en.m.wikipedia.org/wiki/Copy_editing

Writers and Editors: Kinds of editors and levels of edit - what every writer and editor should know (updated)
https://www.writersandeditors.com/blog/posts/33254

British versus American English

American English: Teaching the four skills
https://americanenglish.state.gov/four-skills-resources

Boredpanda: British English vs American English: 24 differences illustrated
https://www.boredpanda.com/british-american-english-differences-language/

Podcasts

bookcareers Live
https://www.bookcareers.com/category/podcasts/

The Book Editor Show
https://podcasters.spotify.com/pod/show/the-book-editor-show

The Copwriter Club Podcast
https://thecopywriterclub.com/podcast/

Delibrate Freelancer
https://meledits.com/category/podcast/

The Editing Podcast
https://www.louiseharnbyproofreader.com/podcast.html

Quick and Dirty Tips for Better Writing
https://open.spotify.com/show/3gRQiaxv3M01MxxBIMxkAy

The Writer Files
https://open.spotify.com/show/56ZG2S92lm2sNeB8JdqLJ5

Katie Wolf
https://www.thekatiewolf.com/podcast/

Directory of book publishing and typesetting companies

https://editorsessentials.com/typesetters-in-india/

https://www.publishersglobal.com/directory/india/media/book-publishers/2

https://www.fiponline.org/members-companies/

APPs AND SOFTWARE FOR COPYEDITORS

Grammar

Grammarly
https://app.grammarly.com/

PerfectIt
https://intelligentediting.com/

Writing

Antidote
https://www.antidote.info/en/

AutoCrit
https://www.autocrit.com/

ProWritingAid
https://prowritingaid.com/

Spelling

1Checker
http://www.1checker.com/

Ginger
https://www.gingersoftware.com/

SlickWrite
https://www.slickwrite.com/#!home

Webspellchecker
https://webspellchecker.com/

Proofreading

ProofreadBot
http://proofreadbot.com/

Plagiarism checking

Dupli checker
https://www.duplichecker.com/

Grammarly Business
https://www.grammarly.com/business

Help.PlagTracker.com
https://help.plagtracker.com/

Plagiarism checker
https://plagiarismcheck.org/

Quetext
https://www.quetext.com/

Turnitin
https://www.turnitin.com/

Citing and referencing

BibGuru
https://www.bibguru.com/

BibMe
https://www.bibme.org/

Citation Machine
https://www.citationmachine.net/

Citavi
https://www.citavi.com/en

Citefast
https://www.citefast.com

CiteThisForMe
https://www.citethisforme.com/

Crossref
https://www.crossref.org/

Docear
https://docear.org/

Easybib
https://www.easybib.com/

Zotero
https://www.zotero.org/

Associations of copyeditors

ACES: The Society for Copyediting
https://aceseditors.org/

Association of Freelance Editors, Proofreaders and Indexers of Ireland (AFEPI Ireland)
https://afepi-ireland.com/

Bay Area Editors Forum
http://www.editorsforum.org/

Board of Editors in the Life Sciences (BELS)
https://www.bels.org/

Canberra Society of Editors
https://www.editorscanberra.org/

Chartered Institute of Editing and Proofreading (CIEP)
https://www.ciep.uk/

Council of Science Editors (CSE)
https://www.councilscienceeditors.org/

Eastern Mediterranean Association of Medical Editors (EMAME)
https://www.emro.who.int/emame/about/

Editorial Freelancers Association (EfA)
https://www.the-efa.org/

Editors Canada
https://www.editors.ca/

Editors' and Proofreaders' Alliance of Northern Ireland (EPANI)
https://www.epani.org.uk/

European Association of Science Editors (EASE)
https://ease.org.uk/

Indian Copyeditors Forum
https://www.facebook.com/groups/Indianeditors/

Institute of Professional Editors (IPEd)
https://www.iped-editors.org/Accreditation

International Society of Managing and Technical Editors (ISMTE)
https://www.ismte.org/default.aspx

Mediterranean Editors and Translators (MET)
https://www.metmeetings.org/

Professional Editors' Guild
https://editors.org.za/#

San Diego Professional Editors Network
https://sdpen.com/

Society for Advancing Business Editing and Writing (SABEW)
https://sabew.org/

Society of Editors (Queensland)
https://editorsqld.com/

Society of Editors South Australia
http://www.editors-sa.org.au/

Society of Editors (WA) (Editors WA)
http://ww1.editorswa.com/

Society of English-Language Professionals in the Netherlands (SENSE)
https://www.sense-online.nl/

Acknowledgements

First of all, I thank the late Karen Judd, author of *Copyediting: a practical guide*, and Wendanyl Nicholos, editor of the *Copyediting* newsletter (the newsletter was subsequently bought by ACES: The Society for Editing), both of whom reviewed the synopsis and the proposed contents of the book way back in 2009 when the idea first possessed me. Their positive comments on the proposed contents and the synopsis helped me take this book forward.

Next, I thank all the authors of this book who took time out from their busy schedules and wrote chapters for us pro bono. (The funds generated by the sales of the book will be used to build the ICF website and brand.) I know some of the authors only online, but it feels as if I have known them for years. Editors from India, the United States, the United Kingdom, and Canada have contributed chapters to this book. Some of our colleagues could not help us out with this book, but we are sure that they would love to be part of the forthcoming books in this series.

I provided only the idea (the seed) and part of a chapter for this project. It is the authors who provided the raw material, and the editorial committee that worked day and night to first review the proposals and then the first and second drafts of chapters, who deserve all the credit. Special thanks to the chair of the committee,

Abha Thapalyal Gandhi, for her tireless work in writing the introductory chapter, reviewing proposals and drafts of chapters, and then writing feedback e-mails (reading those e-mails would indeed be a master class in how to share feedback).

Murugaraj Shanmugam contributed a chapter and played a very important part by sharing his ideas for the book and providing constructive comments on the chapters. Preeta Priyamvada too devoted a lot of time to review the chapters. She also gave valuable suggestions for structuring the content and helped in necessary business-related decisions. Anupam Choudhury helped with surveys and questionnaires used for drafting chapters, and he was absolutely merciless in his reviews. The positive impact of the committee's comments is to be felt throughout the book but not seen.

I thank Malobika Chakraborty and Divya Munjal, who helped us with project management in the earlier stages of the project, and Meenakshi Venkat, who did developmental editing for two chapters of this book and also suggested that we split the book into two (The initial proposal was for 32 chapters!) I thank Shalini Munjal for compiling a list of companies that take copyeditors as interns. I also thank Shweta Bharti Dayal for reviewing the alt text chapter and Vivekanandan Sekar for reviewing the indexing chapter. I thank P K Jayanthan for creating the index and for also doing the final proofreading of the book. Finally, how can I forget to thank Yateendra Joshi, who copyedited the book.

I thank Jyotirmoy Chaudhuri for sharing our book idea with Manish Purohit. A special thanks to our publisher Manish Purohit, who believed in our idea and published this book.

Editorial Committee

Abha Thapalyal Gandhi (Chair)

Abha (abhatgandhi@yahoo.co.in) began her career as a law professional and then was fortunate enough to be introduced to publishing. Currently she is a publishing consultant and freelance editor in the social sciences and humanities. She has also worked as Director, Legal & Regulatory, LexisNexis India; Publisher, South Asia Press; Sr Commissioning Editor, Oxford University Press India; and Sr Legal Editor, *Supreme Court Cases*, EBC India.

Anupam Choudhury

Anupam Choudhury is an independent editor and writer. He is a senior publishing professional with over 14 years of experience in academic publishing. He has previously headed editorial teams at Sage Publications India and Oxford University Press India. His website is www.anupamchoudhury.com

Murugaraj Shanmugam

Murugaraj Shanmugam is the founder-director of Tholga Publishing Services, which he established after working for 18 years with major typesetting companies in India, setting up and managing their copyediting teams. He specializes in academic editing; teaches copyediting through Editor's Essentials (https://editorsessentials.com/), the training arm of Tholga Publishing Services; and mentors copyeditors. As an active member of the Indian Copyeditors Forum, he has delivered many webinars on language and Microsoft Word for editors.

Preeta Priyamvada

Preeta Priyamvada (preeta.edit@gmail.com) is an independent editor. She has 15 years of experience in the publishing industry. She has worked on textbooks, coffee-table books, trade books, and also magazines, journals, and encyclopaedias. Her last assignment was with Pearson as Managing Editor – Development, for academic and trade and higher education social sciences textbooks.

More About ICF

ICF encourages freelance and full-time editors (necessarily Indian, although exceptions can be made in rare cases) to engage in active networking and hopes to create a culture of meaningful and sustained interaction. The forum invites editors to share success stories and problems of freelancing, provide leads, warn (always discreetly), ask questions, and discuss editorial bugbears including oddly written sentences and other professional concerns.

In addition to editors, the ICF welcomes abstractors, designers, indexers, manuscript evaluators, project managers, proofreaders, translators, typesetters, authors, and content writers.

The forum has a website (indiancopyeditors.wixsite.com/copyeditor) and a Google group and is also on Twitter (Indianeditors), LinkedIn (https://www.linkedin.com/groups/8413786/), and Pinterest (https://in.pinterest.com/indianeditors/boards/).

Check out the ICF WIN series: webinars (webinars on the craft of editing), interviews with editing professionals (on the business side of editing), and the best of nature (the travel series Break-Free) on our YouTube channel. Videos and recordings of all sessions are available at youtube.com/c/IndianCopyeditorsForum to anyone.

The table that follows gives a listing of our groups on WhatsApp.

Community-specific groups	Location-specific groups		Theme-based groups
Journal Editors	Delhi NCR	Mangalore	Jobs Senior Editors
Legal Editors	Pune	India	Early Career Editors
Book Editors	Maharashtra/Mumbai	International	Business Mentorship
Translators	Thane/Navi Mumbai	Singapore	Editing Certification
Poetry Editors	TN/Chennai/Pondy	Goa/Panaji	Learning and Resources (for training)
Hindi Editors	Karnataka/Bengaluru	Punjab/Chandigarh	Webinars
Prepress and Postpress	West Bengal/Kolkata	Himachal/Shimla	Associations' Members (for Indian members of foreign editing associations)
Content Writers	AP/Hyderabad	Kerala/Thiruvananthapuram	Mentorship
Macros	Tricity (Chandigarh/Mohali/Panchkula)	Haryana/Chandigarh	Promotions and Blogs
Beta Readers	Madhya Pradesh/Bhopal	Odisha/Bhubaneshwar	Travel Diaries
Fiction Editors	Jharkhand/Ranchi	Uttar Pradesh/Lucknow	Editing Courses
Digital Services	Rajasthan/Jaipur	Bihar/Patna	Handbooks for Editors
	Uttarakhand/Dehra Dun	Canada/Toronto	Book Club
	Northeast	Mysuru	
	Gujarat/Ahmedabad	J&K/Srinagar	

In posting to the discussion forum on Facebook and WhatsApp, please use the following tags:

#jobopft for full-time jobs
#joboppt for part-time jobs
#jobopf for freelance gigs
#news
#tools
#query
#meetings
#tests
#certifications

As of 30 May 2023, ICF members have met 115 times in 27 cities (Bengaluru, Bhopal, Chandigarh, Chennai, Dehra Dun, Delhi, Ghaziabad, Gurgaon, Hyderabad, Jaipur, Kolkata, Lucknow, Mandwa, Modinagar, Mumbai, Navi Mumbai, Noida, Panaji, Panchkula, Pondicherry, Pune, Ranchi, Solan, Singapore, Srinagar, Thiruvananthapuram, and Vadodara). ICF members also meet online through videoconferences and meetings.

India offers a large pool of wonderful editorial talent to the world, so let's get it together to display our high editorial standards and promote freelance and full-time editors as professionals in their own right. Do join us at facebook.com/groups/Indianeditors.

Index

S

T